THE HOMESTEADER'S GUIDE TO GROWING HERBS

THE HOMESTEADER'S GUIDE TO GROWING HERBS

Learn to Grow, Prepare, and Use Herbs

For Your Family and Livestock

Kristine Brown, RH (AHG)

ILLUSTRATIONS BY MARY WOODIN

ROCKRIDGE PRESS

For general information on our other products and services or to obtain technical support, please contact our Customer Care Department within the United States at (866) 744-2665, or outside the United States at (510) 253-0500.

Rockridge Press publishes its books in a variety of electronic and print formats. Some content that appears in print may not be available in electronic books, and vice versa.

Interior and Cover Designer: Diana Haas
Art Producer: Tom Hood
Editor: Marjorie DeWitt
Production Editor: Chris Gage

Illustrations © Mary Woodin, 2020. Photography Yuliya Koshchiy/Shutterstock, p. 24; Heliosphile/Shutterstock, p. 26; Spok83/Shutterstock, p. 28; Przemyslaw Muszynski/Shutterstock, p. 30; JRP Studio/Shutterstock, p. 32; Anastasiia Malinich/Shutterstock, p. 34; Cornelia Pithart/Shutterstock, p. 36; sopon seti/Shutterstock, p. 38; sripfoto/Shutterstock, p. 40; Manfred Ruckszio/Shutterstock, p. 42; encierro/Shutterstock, p. 44; motorolka/Shutterstock, p. 46; yevgeniy11/Shutterstock, p. 48; Roxana Bashyrova/Shutterstock, p.50; Olga Shum/Shutterstock, p. 52; c12/Shutterstock, p. 54; HandmadePictures/Shutterstock, p. 56; Inga Nielsen/Shutterstock, p. 58; weha/Shutterstock, p. 60; Koxae Sun/Shutterstock, p. 62.

ISBN: Print 978-1-64739-372-4 | eBook 978-1-64739-373-1
R0

To my partner, Greg, for indulging me in
my crazy scheme to grow a homestead.

CONTENTS

||||||||||||||||||||||||||||||||||||||||||||||||||||

INTRODUCTION

From the age of two, I was raised on a farm. We had 14 acres, which included a pond and pasture; fruit trees, such as sour cherries, apples, apricots, peaches, and nectarines; plus a small grape arbor and gooseberry bushes. We had English walnut, black walnut, and hazelnut bushes as well. My parents grew many vegetables, and we canned or froze many foods throughout the year.

We had horses, and we also usually had two steers in the pasture, which we raised and butchered for meat. We had a few dozen chickens always scattered about the barnyard, and raising fluffy little chicks into full-grown hens was an annual practice.

So when my partner and I were looking for a home where we could combine and raise our two existing families and our newly growing family, it was natural that I wanted to give our children a similar upbringing as I had. We found a small farm. So small, in fact, that I wasn't allowed to say it was a farm—we dubbed it "the farmette."

We've never raised any cattle, but our little homestead boasted sheep, goats, chickens, turkeys, ducks, and bees in its prime. We wanted to be as self-subsistent as possible, and considering we were pretty poor at the time, growing our own food meant we could have the wholesome foods that lack of money prevented us from buying at the grocery store.

What we didn't grow I often bartered for at the local farmers' market with my handmade soap and my raw goat milk. Sales from these items also helped us purchase grass-fed beef.

As an herbalist, growing herbs on my homestead was a given. Each spring I would eagerly start herb seeds in my greenhouse, growing a variety of medicinal herbs to be used around our homestead. Each year, it was a challenge to try to find another spot to tuck yet another new variety of herb while maintaining enough room for the existing herbs to grow.

We lived as naturally as possible, out of preference and necessity. This also extended to how we raised our animals. Through trial and error—and often out of necessity—I learned what herbs worked great with animals (and which ones not so much), and a dozen or so herbs became the mainstay for our animals' good health.

Though we have scaled back our homestead gardens in the past few years due to exhaustion and lack of time, I still have many wild and weedy herb gardens. One of my favorite things to do in the early morning is to walk among my herbs, picking a leaf here and there to brew in my morning cup of tea. To these plants I owe my family's and my own health; over the years they have nurtured and supported us through many mishaps and illnesses and kept us healthy.

This book is like a quick stroll through my herb garden. Although I've only got room to discuss a handful of herbs and recipes, I've highlighted those that will be a strong cornerstone of your herbal arsenal.

CHAPTER ONE

WHY GROW HERBS?

In this chapter, I discuss the benefits of growing your own herbs. I address safety issues to help reduce any fears you might have, go over the differences between conventional and herbal medicine and when to use each, give you a brief history of herbalism, and provide my top 10 ways to use herbs every day.

BENEFITS OF HERBS ON THE HOMESTEAD

There are many benefits of growing herbs on your homestead. You can grow the herbs needed for your food and medicinal requirements at a fraction of the cost of purchasing those same herbs from a reputable source. Growing your own herbs ensures that you are getting the freshest and highest quality herbs available. Excess plants that are weeded out can become compost or fertilizer. They can also enrich the diet of your livestock by providing extra nutrition and an immune system boost. Herbs also make great companion plants to many of your existing vegetables and fruit trees.

Just as you may harvest vegetables daily for your meals, you'll soon be harvesting fresh herbs to add to those meals, not only improving their flavor but increasing their nutritional and medicinal value as well. Think of the many herbs you find in the spice cabinet, such as sage, rosemary, thyme, and garlic. While they add great flavors to all kinds of foods, they also have an array of medicinal and nutritive benefits, such as providing a natural source of vitamins and minerals.

SAFETY

Are you feeling a bit nervous about using herbs? Have you been warned of potential dangers and side effects of taking herbs? I'm here to assure you that when used wisely, herbal medicine is as dangerous as eating a salad with your dinner. The majority of herbs can be consumed in large amounts before causing any side effects, just like the fruits and vegetables you grow in your garden, making them safe and reliable sources of natural medicine. Unlike many conventional medications, these herbs have few, if any, side effects. A few herbs can cause problems if ingested in too large a quantity. If this happens, discontinuing use generally stops any unwanted effects fairly quickly. Always do your research before using herbs, and make sure you have positively identified the herb before using it.

WHAT IS HERBALISM?

Herbalism is the use of plants for medicine. As unusual as it may sound in our modern world, herbs are the original medicine. A variety of herbs have been found on the remains of a cave dweller in Iraq dating back 60,000 years. Seven of the herbs seen on those remains are still in use today as herbal medicine.

Throughout time, herbs were the main source of healing until harsher medicines caught on, including arsenic and mercury. Chemists became fascinated with the chemical components of herbs and sought to isolate constituents to try to create better medicine. And although the approach may seem better, many times chemists don't take into account why a plant has the variety of constituents that it does. These combinations often work together in ways that chemists don't understand. We can benefit from these combinations by using whole-plant medicine to make a variety of herbal remedies.

By using whole-plant remedies (which can consist of using the entire plant or just parts, such as the leaves, stems, flowers, bark, or seeds), we can make tinctures, syrups, salves, teas, and more to help boost our health and heal minor cuts and scrapes. Adding these same plants to the foods you prepare can help add nutrition and boost your immune system.

CONVENTIONAL VS. HERBAL REMEDIES

When starting out with medicinal herbs, you might be tempted to think that herbs can fully replace conventional medicine. And while they can in some instances, especially when used in combination with a healthy diet, exercise, and getting plenty of sleep, there are times when conventional medicine is still needed. In acute situations, such as a heart attack, there is no substitute for the life-saving help a hospital can give, whereas herbs would be better used as support on the road to recovery. Always seek the advice of a health care professional before using herbs for a medical condition.

TOP 10 WAYS TO USE HERBS IN YOUR DAILY LIFE

What's the best way to get started? Try incorporating a few of these ideas into your daily life as easy ways to use herbs.

1. Use herbs to flavor food.

2. Use herbs to enhance your livestock's daily nutrition with fresh greens that are both nutritious and immune boosting.

3. Use herbs to make teas and infusions that are full of vitamins and minerals to keep you and your family healthy.

4. Use herbs to help build up the compost and fertilize other plants.

5. Use herbs to help keep your home clean and germ free.

6. Use herbs as medicine for a variety of aches, pains, bumps, or bruises.

7. Use herbs as great companion plants with other plants in your gardens.

8. Use herbs to help preserve meats and cheeses.

9. Use herbs to keep insects and other pests away.

10. Use herbs to make your home smell fresh and clean.

CHAPTER TWO

PLANNING YOUR HERB GARDEN

In this chapter, I give you the tools you need to create a plan for your herb garden. I go over how to choose the right herbs for your homestead to help take the guesswork out of what you need. I discuss the requirements for a garden space, including the location, size, type of soil, and growing conditions needed. I also talk about container gardening in case you are homesteading on a small plot of land or cannot plant in the ground. Finally, because the weeds that grow all around us are often types of herbs, I touch briefly on foraging for herbs as well.

SELECTING YOUR HERBS

You may be wondering where to start. What herbs should you plant in your homestead garden? How many of them should you plant? This can be a daunting task, but I'll help you break it down easily. Grab a pen and paper so you can start making a list.

First off, think of all the herbs you generally use in your meals. Some examples are garlic, onion, thyme, sage, rosemary, basil, and peppermint. Most of the mint family plants multiply very readily, so you need only one or two of each of these plants, depending on your space. You need a larger number of onion and garlic plants, and you can plant these in regular garden rows or in raised beds. I typically calculate one bulb of each per day of the year, so around 365 of each. Adjust these numbers according to your usage.

Next, start considering herbs you'll use medicinally. Keep in mind that this list will change with your needs. You want to grow a variety of medicinal herbs that are versatile and address your family's needs. Some all-purpose medicinal herbs to grow include motherwort, lavender, chamomile, Saint John's wort, elderberry, and comfrey. Look over the herb profiles in chapter 4 for additional ideas that may be useful to you.

Some herbs, like the kitchen-friendly herbs, can be used both for cooking and for medicine. These dual-purpose herbs are great because the flavors are often familiar, so turning them into medicine won't be hard on your taste buds.

To get a better idea of the herbs you may need, look through the ailment index (page 164) for ailments that are common in your household and see which herbs are listed in the recipes and remedies provided.

Now that you've got a list started, you need to sketch your garden plan and locate the herbs according to their needs. The individual needs for the herbs listed in this book can be found in their profiles in chapter 4. Read on for more ideas on the location and size of your garden.

LOCATION AND SIZE

The location and amount of space you have for your garden will help determine what you can grow. Do you have an acre or more to dedicate to your homestead garden? If so, you probably have more than enough space to grow an herb garden within your general garden area. Keep in mind that some herbs prefer part sun to shade, whereas others thrive in full sun, just like your vegetables. Is your garden space limited? Then you might need to be creative about tucking away a few herbs here and there among your vegetables.

Let's dive a bit deeper into these factors.

Where Should You Grow?

Let's talk about location. As a homesteader, you most likely have several acres to choose from when growing your plants. Since different herbs have different environmental needs, it's great if you have both sunny and shady locations to plant in.

I like to look at growing from a permaculture standpoint (i.e., planting herbs for every-day use closer to the house while planting those that are harvested only occasionally, such as willow trees that are harvested from only once or twice a year, around the perimeter). If you have a larger homestead, keep this in mind when designing your gardens. If you have already established a vegetable garden, you may wish to incorporate your herb garden in a section of that garden.

While many herbs such as thyme, basil, lavender, and oregano prefer to grow in full sun, some such as stinging nettles can thrive in a partly sunny to shady location, as well as full sun. Assess your property and decide what you have available. If you are home-steading on a small plot, an acre or less, you may choose to supplement your planting area by adding plants in containers on your patio or in window boxes on a side of your house that receives a lot of sun.

Even with a small space you can grow a lot of herbs to nourish and heal your family, pets, and livestock. A few containers, window boxes, or even an herb spiral (an area that builds up while spiraling to accommodate many plants in a small space) can supply you with almost all the herbs you might need for a year or more.

When planting trees on your homestead, be sure to plant a variety to give you the maximum amount of food and medicine possible. For instance, instead of planting five oak trees, try planting one oak tree and four other trees, such as willow, hawthorn, black walnut, and mimosa trees. This would give quite a variety of medicine while also giving you the shade you desire for your homestead.

Be sure to either fence in your garden or fence in your livestock, so you don't lose your entire herb patch to an unruly herd of goats or a flock of chickens.

CONTAINER GARDENS

If you find yourself in a space where you don't have a lot of land to grow on, you can grow herbs in containers. Many herbs adapt well to containers on a patio or along the driveway. Be sure that your containers drain well and are located in the amount of sun or shade that your plants need.

Containers are great for plants in the mint family, even if you do have enough space to grow them in the ground, because these plants tend to be a bit rowdy and can take over the space they are growing in. Keeping your peppermint, lemon balm, and catnip tucked away in a container is a sure way to save the garden space for plants that won't compete with each other as much.

Using containers, you can also grow upward. Add a trellis so that climbing herbs such as passionflower or hops grow upward, allowing for better growth and easier harvest.

Containers also allow you to control water and fertilizing with ease. With the added bonus of being located right outside your door, container plants often get attention that general garden plants do not.

How Much Space Do You Need?

The eternal question of the homesteader is: How much space do I need to grow a garden? The answer depends on how much you want to grow. The great thing about herbs is that they don't take up a lot of space—although they will if you let them—so you can still grow herbs, even if you have limited space available.

My advice is to start small. It's easy to get carried away and plant more than you can manage. While herbs can be very forgiving, you need to do maintenance to keep competing weeds out of their area. If you've ever studied square-foot gardening, you know that you can cram a lot into a little space.

Herbs are typically planted 12 to 18 inches apart, but if you plant them closer together (8 to 12 inches) to conserve space, they will adapt. If you plant them too close together (less than 6 to 8 inches), some herbs may grow stunted, whereas others such as mints and stinging nettles will simply crowd out their competitors.

While it may seem that it's possible to have too small of a garden and impossible to have too big of one, having a space too large can be just as bad as having a space too small. If you plant too much and you're not familiar with gardening, it is easy to get discouraged after the rainy season passes and leaves you with more weeds than you can physically remove from your garden. I like the permaculture method of gardening and use many of the concepts, such as including a layer of cardboard followed by heavy mulching to keep down the weeds.

When starting your herb garden, take your experience into consideration along with the amount of time you have to commit to your garden and the needs you have for the herbs. Many herbs are perennials, so if you aren't able to harvest them, they will often return the following year, giving you another chance to harvest. A few herbs, such as chamomile, calendula, and basil, are annuals, so they have to be replanted each year.

Let's talk size. A small 3-foot-by-6-foot bed can give you enough space to plant about two dozen herbs or roughly 160 onions or garlic plants. Doubling that space gives you nearly a year's supply of onions or garlic or four dozen herbs. When creating beds, allow for 3 feet of space between them to give you ample room to move between the beds and for plants to spill out over the edges.

FORAGING HERBS

Many of the medicinal plants we use are considered to be weeds and can be readily found growing in the wild. These plants are typically high in nutrients as they get to pick their location for growth, allowing them to select their favored growing conditions. However, they are not picky, so if you are harvesting plants from the wild, make sure they are not growing in a contaminated area. Never harvest plants growing near a roadside or in a drainage ditch that contains runoff from agricultural crops, since they are often drawing up all the toxic fumes and pesticides from their surroundings.

Never harvest an at-risk plant from the wild. For more information on avoiding at-risk plants, see the resources section (page 157). Plants that are great for foraging include elderberry, stinging nettles, wild lettuce, plantain, dandelion, violet, turkey tail, reishi, maitake, wild cherry, oak, pine, and blackberry. Depending on your location, the variety of plants available can vary, so check your local resources to find out what plants grow near you.

SOIL AND SEEDS

Many herbs can thrive in a variety of soils, but if you can, try to amend your soil to be a rich loam. Clay can often hold water near the roots, which can waterlog a plant, whereas sand will drain away any moisture. If you have clay, your ground will be hard to dig in and you may have standing water in your garden area. Sandy soil will be dry and loose, with a dusty look to it. You can either amend your soil by adding compost or manure or both to the soil the fall before you begin your garden, or practice a lasagna garden method to help build up your soil. The lasagna garden method consists of layering: Start with a layer of cardboard, add a layer of leaves, followed by a layer of compost or manure, and top with a layer of mulch. As the materials break down, they will add nutrients to the soil and give a nice crumbly mix that plants adore.

Another way to get better soil is to build raised beds using logs or landscape lumber. Lay down a few layers of heavy cardboard, then fill them with compost, manure, grass clippings, leaves, and so on to build up the space.

Once your garden is prepared, you are ready to start planting. There are a lot of great resources for herb seeds online; look in the resources section (page 157) for my favorite choices. You may also be able to find a limited amount of herb seeds at your local farm supply store. Look for organic seeds when possible.

ONWARD TO GROWING

This chapter was a brief overview on getting your herb garden started. You should now feel a bit more comfortable with growing herbs in your garden. More in-depth information on growing specific herbs can be found in chapter 4 in the individual herb profiles.

CHAPTER THREE

HERBAL PREPARATIONS

In this chapter, I talk about my preferred essential tools for creating herbal medicine. I also provide a rundown of some of the more popular methods of preparing herbs and how they are made. I go over teas and the differences between decoctions and infusions, syrups, tinctures, poultices, and oils and salves. This section builds the foundation for the recipes in the later chapters, so you'll want to book-mark it for easy reference when it comes time to make the recipes.

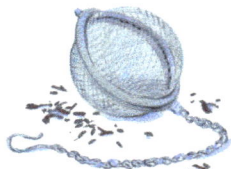

THE TOOLS OF THE TRADE

Here is a short list of the tools I find to be essential.

- **GLASS JARS** of all sizes—to economize, save your empty glass food jars

- **GLASS MEASURING CONTAINERS** in 1-cup, 2-cup, and 4-cup sizes

- **DROPPER BOTTLES** in 1-ounce, 2-ounce, and 4-ounce sizes, preferably amber or cobalt

- **DOUBLE BOILER** or a saucepan and fitted bowl or glass measuring container

- **SHARP KNIVES OR ULU** for chopping up fresh herbs and roots

- **CUTTING BOARD** to cut your herbs on

- **SPATULAS AND LADLES** for stirring and pouring

- **TEA BALL, MUSLIN BAGS, OR ANOTHER TEA INFUSER** for infusing tea

- **CHEESECLOTH OR OTHER THIN FABRIC** for straining off herbal infusions

- **COFFEE FILTERS** also make nice strainers for herbs with fine hairs, such as mullein and rose hips

- **LABELS** to label your remedies

- **MEASURING CUPS AND SPOONS** for measuring out ingredients

- **STICK OR IMMERSION BLENDER** for blending oils into creams

- **WAX PAPER** to protect metal lids from vinegar infusions

- **SCALE** for measuring ingredients such as beeswax and cocoa butter

- **FUNNEL**, preferably a small metal one to make it easier for pouring tinctures into bottles

- **LATEX GLOVES** to protect hands from black walnut hulls

- **GARDEN GLOVES** to protect hands from stinging nettles during harvesting

- **DRYING SCREENS, A DEHYDRATOR, OR BOTH** to dry your herbs for storage

- **EYE CUP** for eye washes

TEAS (DECOCTIONS AND INFUSIONS)

Tea is a loose term to describe making an herbal drink with water. A general tea can be steeped, or it can be infused or decocted. Infusions steep a large quantity of leaves, flowers, and aerial parts over a long period of time, whereas decoctions are reserved for tougher plant parts, such as roots, seeds, and barks, and are simmered for a short period of time.

How to Make It

Tea

1. Boil water in a tea kettle.

2. While the water is heating up, measure 1 to 2 teaspoons of dried herbs, put it in a tea ball or muslin bag, and put that in your teacup for a single cup or in a pot for multiple cups.

3. Pour 8 to 10 ounces boiling water into the cup or pot, and steep for 15 to 20 minutes.

Infusion

1. Measure 1 cup of dried herbs for every quart of water you'll be adding, and put it in the appropriate jar (quart jar, half-gallon jar, gallon jar).

2. Put a large metal spoon in the jar (this helps keep the jar from cracking).

3. Boil the appropriate amount of water and then pour it into the jar with the herbs.

4. Let steep for 6 to 8 hours.

5. Strain the herbs, return the liquid to the jar, cover, and refrigerate. Compost the herbs.

6. Drink cold, at room temperature, or heated up within 4 days.

Decoction

1. Measure 1 to 4 tablespoons of dried herbs and put them in a saucepan.

2. Pour 12 to 16 ounces of water into the saucepan with the herbs.

3. Bring the water to a boil over high heat, then reduce the heat to medium-low and simmer for 20 to 45 minutes.

4. Strain the herbs, pour the liquid into a quart jar, cover, and refrigerate. Compost the herbs.

5. Drink cold, at room temperature, or heated up within 4 days.

SYRUP

Syrups are a great way to get kids to take their medicine. They are great for soothing sore throats and coughs, and they can make a great herbal soda. Syrups are fairly easy to create by brewing an herbal infusion, then slowly thickening it by adding honey or sugar.

How to Make It

Basic Syrup

1. Make a strong tea by putting about ½ cup of dried herbs into a saucepan with 16 ounces of water.

2. Over high heat, bring the water to a boil, then turn off the heat and steep for 15 to 30 minutes.

3. Strain and return the tea to the saucepan. Compost the herbs.

4. Add 1 cup of sugar (or half the amount of water that you used), and slowly heat over medium-low heat until the liquid is reduced by half. Do not let your tea boil. You want to slowly evaporate the water. For instance, if you have 2 cups of tea, add 1 cup of sugar to the pan, and cook down to 1 cup total. (If you are adding honey, there is no need to cook down the formula. Simply add 1 cup of honey and stir it into the tea. If you want a thicker syrup, add more honey.)

5. Store your syrup covered in the refrigerator. Syrups generally last 3 to 6 months.

TINCTURE

A tincture is one of the most efficient ways to make an herbal remedy, combining a small amount of plant material with a menstruum, or solvent, such as alcohol, vinegar, or glycerite. They are portable, store easily in a bottle, and are shelf stable, generally lasting many years.

How to Make It

Alcohol Tincture

1. Put chopped fresh herbs or dried herbs in a glass jar. The amount will vary according to the herb, so check the herbal monographs in chapter 4 for specific amounts.

2. Add alcohol and water according to the monograph instructions. Since the alcohol content varies by herb, you will notice in the herb profiles that the instructions are given something like this for basil (page 25): Tincture fresh 1:2 or dried 1:4 in 65 percent alcohol. This means to fill any size jar with one part of the fresh herb to two parts menstruum (or one part of the dried herb to four parts menstruum) and add a solution of 65 percent alcohol and 35 percent water. So for an 8-ounce jar, you would fill your jar halfway with fresh herb, then pour grain alcohol to fill it about 65 percent full, then top off with water.

3. Secure the lid on the jar and let steep for 4 to 6 weeks, shaking daily. At the end of the steeping period, strain the plant material, reserving the liquid, and compost or leave it in the jar. (I prefer to leave harder materials, such as seeds, roots, and bark, in my tinctures indefinitely because the medicinal properties extract even more over time.) Most tinctures keep indefinitely as long as they are stored in a dark location.

Glycerite Tincture

1. Begin the same way as for alcohol—by adding herbs to a jar. Glycerites don't usually extract as strongly as alcohol, so fill your jar half full of plant material.

2. Add glycerin to fill the jar half full again, then top off with water.

3. Let steep for 4 to 6 weeks, shaking daily.

4. Strain the plant material, reserving the liquid, and compost. Store the tincture in a cool, dark location. Glycerites generally last 1 to 2 years.

Vinegar Tincture

1. Put fresh or dried herbs in your jar. If using fresh, loosely fill half a jar; for dried, fill one-quarter full.

2. Top off with apple cider vinegar.

3. Place a piece of wax paper over the mouth of the jar before sealing the lid.

4. Let steep for 2 to 4 weeks, shaking daily.

5. Strain the plant material, reserving the liquid, and compost (or add the plant material to salads for a tangy addition). Vinegars typically last several years.

POULTICES

A poultice is an application of fresh or dried herbs that are applied directly to a wound. It can be simple, such as a spit poultice, which is a fresh herb chewed up, spit out, and placed on the wound or it can use herbs chopped and broken down with hot water.

How to Make It

Basic Poultice

1. Make a tea using freshly chopped fresh herbs or dried herbs.

2. After the herbs have steeped for a few minutes, strain the herbs, reserving the liquid for drinking.

3. Cover the herbs with a soft cloth, such as flannel, and bind to the body with a stretch bandage.

4. Leave on for several hours or overnight.

5. Reapply once or twice a day.

OILS AND SALVES

An herbal infused oil is made by steeping herbs in an oil, similar to making a tea or a tincture. Herbal infused oils are not the same as essential oils, which are composed of specific constituents that are separated from the plant. Rather, they can be made from any type of oil, and often the oil is paired with an intended use, such as almond oil as a massage oil, or castor oil as a drawing oil. Oils can be applied externally or used internally and are a great way to infuse herbs into your food. They are great when you need deep penetration of herbs into the skin, such as for a sprain or pulled muscle.

Herbal salves are infused oils that have been thickened, generally with beeswax. They are less messy than oils and are great for applying herbs to cuts, burns, and other skin afflictions. They tend to hold the herbs close to the surface of the skin, unlike oils that are easily absorbed for deep penetration.

How to Make It

Herb-Infused Oil

1. Add ½ cup of dried herbs (don't use fresh, since they will introduce water into the oil, causing it to go rancid) to 1½ cups of oil in the top of a double boiler.

2. Add water to the bottom of the double boiler and bring it to a boil over high heat. Immediately reduce the heat to low. (You do not want the herbs and oil to boil continuously.)

3. Gently simmer for 8 to 24 hours, adding water to the bottom as needed. (It is fine to turn off the heat overnight, or if you need to leave the house, just cover the oil with a lid while the heat is off.)

4. Line a strainer with cheesecloth or other light material and strain, reserving the liquid. Do not squeeze the plant material. (You want to avoid introducing any moisture into the oil.)

5. Compost the plant material and let the oil sit undisturbed for 24 hours.

6. Check the oil for a water line. If there is any water, carefully pour off the oil and discard the final portion with water in it.

7. You may wish to add a pinch of slippery elm bark or the contents of a vitamin E gelcap to the oil to help preserve it.

8. Store your oil in the refrigerator, and it will last for about 1 year. If the oil begins to have an off smell, it has gone rancid, and it's time for it to be composted.

Salve

1. Start with an infused oil. You will need 1 ounce of beeswax for every 8 ounces of oil.

2. In a double boiler over high heat, warm the oil and beeswax until the beeswax melts.

3. Once the beeswax has melted, put a few drops on a spoon and let it cool. Test the salve with your finger. If it's too soft, add more wax; if it's too firm, add more oil. Keep in mind the salve will firm up a bit more than it does on the spoon once it has completely set up in your container.

4. Store the salve in an airtight container in a cool, dark location. Salves generally last for 6 months to 1 year. If it begins to have an off smell, it has gone rancid, and it's time for it to be composted.

CHAPTER FOUR

HERBS A TO Z

In this chapter are profiles for 20 common medicinal herbs that are easy to grow on the homestead. Please note that dosage information is based on a 150-pound adult. Adjust dosages for smaller adults, children, and larger adults accordingly. For instance, to administer herbs to a 75-pound child, reduce the dosage by half. Also consider the sensitivity of the person you are giving herbs to. If they normally react easily to medications, start off with a dose that is one-third or one-fourth the normal dose and increase the dose over the course of a week. If any reactions occur, stop using the herbs immediately.

BASIL

Ocimum basilicum

PARTS USED: Aerial parts

USES: Great for digestive issues, including flatulence and bloated stomach after a meal. Stimulates the appetite, helps reduce reaction to gluten and dairy intolerances, reduces headaches, lowers fevers, combats seasonal affective disorder, clears the mind, lowers blood pressure, calms nervous tension, clears excess phlegm from the lungs, freshens breath, cleans teeth and gums, eliminates bacteria, increases flow of milk, stimulates the uterus, and soothes insect stings and bites.

GROWING: An annual plant that grows to a height of about 2 feet. Prefers full sun, well-drained soil, and a fair amount of water. Can tolerate less water once established. A great companion plant to tomatoes. Weed weekly until plants are well established, then weed as needed. To reduce the amount of weeds, mulch heavily with grass clippings. Fertilize with compost at the beginning of the growing season. Pinch back leaves heavily as the plant starts to flower to encourage bushy growth, and harvest as needed.

PREPARATIONS: Tincture fresh 1:2 or dried 1:4 in 65 percent alcohol or make into a standard tea.

SAFETY CONSIDERATIONS: Generally regarded as safe.

DOSAGE: Take 30 drops tincture 3 times a day or 1 to 2 cups of tea daily.

PRESERVATION: Basil can be chopped up and added to ice cubes with a bit of olive oil or water and frozen or whole-leaf dried.

TIP: *There are many great cultivars of basil available; my personal favorite is cinnamon basil. For extra medicinal value, consider also growing tulsi, otherwise known as holy basil, which also has adaptogenic, or stress-reducing, properties.*

BLACK WALNUT

Juglans nigra

PARTS USED: Both green and black hulls, leaf, twig

USES: Great for dispelling parasites, including *Giardia* and many worms; great for external application to fungi such as athlete's foot, jock itch, candida, and ring-worm; useful for viral outbreaks of chicken pox and shingles; soothes inflammatory bowel conditions and hemorrhoids; resolves diarrhea; stops bleeding; helps with recovery from electric shock; and stimulates the central nervous system. Rotten hulls can be used for hypothyroid conditions and goiters.

GROWING: Deciduous trees growing to a height of 80 feet. They tend to grow on the edges of woodlands due to preferring full sun, and they will grow in a variety of soils, including clay, preferring moist soil. Black walnuts repel other plants and trees, so plant them in locations where they won't be crowded. Harvest green hulls as they fall to the ground. Harvest leaves in the spring or summer.

PREPARATIONS: Tincture hulls, chop into pieces 1:2 in 50 percent alcohol or make into a standard oil. Tincture leaf, twig, or both fresh 1:2 in 60 percent alcohol or dried 1:4 in 40 percent alcohol or make into a standard oil.

SAFETY CONSIDERATIONS: Generally regarded as safe.

DOSAGE: Take 30 drops tincture 3 times daily. Apply the oil to ringworm, candida, or other inflictions 2 to 3 times daily.

PRESERVATION: The hulls can be frozen for future use. The leaves can be dried.

TIP: *Use black walnut as a hair dye for a dark brown color. It dyes fabric well, too! Be sure to wear gloves when you are using this herb, as it will stain your hands.*

CHAMOMILE

Matricaria recutita, Anthemis nobilis

PARTS USED: Flower

USES: Relieves all things digestive; calms nervous tension; eases sciatica, neuralgia, and other nerve-related pains; relaxes peripheral nerves and muscles; lessens anxiety; helps with vertigo; soothes bladder inflammation and infection; breaks down kidney stones and gallstones; reduces fevers; eases aches and pains of influenza; relieves colic and teething in babies; eases menstrual-related migraines and cramping; calms false labor pains; lessens night terrors and nightmares; promotes deep sleep; relieves conjunctivitis and soothes irritated eyes; and relieves skin issues including inflammation, fungi, psoriasis, eczema, burning, blisters, radiation burns, acne, and impetigo.

GROWING: German chamomile is an annual plant that grows to a height of 30 inches, whereas Roman chamomile is a perennial growing to a height of 12 inches. Both can be planted as a ground cover that can be walked on. Chamomile prefers well-draining soil, full sun to part shade, with a moderate amount of water—so be sure to water every 3 to 5 days. Weed thoroughly when the plants are getting established, then weed as needed. Fertilize with compost once they are 6 to 8 inches in height. Harvest flowers daily once the plant starts blooming, picking freshly opened blooms in the morning after the dew dries.

PREPARATIONS: Tincture fresh flower 1:2 in 75 percent alcohol or dried flower 1:5 in 50 percent alcohol. Standard infusion of flower for kidney stones and gallstones. Standard tea for internal or external use.

SAFETY CONSIDERATIONS: Generally regarded as safe.

DOSAGE: Take 30 drops tincture 3 times a day or 1 to 2 cups of tea daily. One quart of infusion daily for kidney stones or gallstones. Externally, use as an eye rinse 2 to 3 times daily or a skin rinse or compress 4 to 5 times daily.

PRESERVATION: Dry the flowers on a screen for future use.

TIP: *To harvest a large amount of flowers, use a blueberry picker.*

COMFREY

Symphytum officinale

PARTS USED: Root, leaf

USES: Use the leaf externally to soothe dry, itchy skin; mend broken bones, external ulcers, cuts, and perineal tears; seal wounds (use in combination with an antimicrobial herb such as calendula); and fade age spots. Internally, the leaf is used to heal gastric and duodenal ulcers, ulcerative colitis, leaky gut, and other digestive issues. It reduces coughs from bronchial infections and helps mend broken bones. The root can be used externally to break up scar tissue to reduce or eliminate scars.

GROWING: Perennial herb grows to a height of 4 feet. Prefers to grow in sunny, open spaces but will grow in shade. Comfrey grows in a variety of soil types and once established can be hard to remove, so be sure to plant it where you want it! If any bit of root is left behind, a new plant will grow. Great companion plant to orchard trees to help fertilize them. Weed weekly until plants are established, and you'll most likely never need to weed again. Harvest leaves and roots for medicinal use while the plant is in full flower. Harvest leaves for fertilizer at any time during the growing stage.

PREPARATIONS: Root poultice applied directly to scar tissue to reduce scarring. Tea of ¼ cup leaf to 8 ounces of boiling water, steeped 20 minutes for compress on external issues or standard tea for internal issues.

SAFETY CONSIDERATIONS: Do not use internally during pregnancy or lactation. Do not use with a history of liver conditions or in combination with heavy alcohol consumption. Use the leaf internally for a short term (2 to 4 weeks) only. Never use the root internally.

DOSAGE: Root poultice and leaf compresses applied 3 to 6 times daily, not to exceed 6 weeks. One cup of tea daily, not to exceed 4 weeks.

PRESERVATION: Wash and chop the roots for drying. Dry the leaves whole, then crumble lightly to store.

TIP: *Grow only the purple-flowered comfrey for medicine and avoid the yellow-flowered species as it has more pyrrolizidine alkaloids.*

ECHINACEA

Echinacea purpurea

PARTS USED: Aerial parts, roots

USES: Used for septicemia and septic infections. Clears stagnant lymph; boosts immune system function to ward off colds, influenza, sore throats, sinus infections, bronchitis, arthritis, fevers, and candida overgrowth; inhibits tumor growth; preserves white blood cells; eases mastitis; and reduces thrush.

GROWING: Echinacea is a perennial that grows to a height of 3 feet, preferring full sun, and grows in a variety of soils. Echinacea is drought tolerant. Plant in a garden to attract pollinators. Weed weekly until established when echinacea will provide enough cover to eliminate most weed growth. Apply Comfrey Fertilizer (page 125) or compost once a year in the early spring. Harvest roots in the spring or fall after the growth has died back. Harvest the aerial parts during flowering and seed stages to get both flowers and seeds.

PREPARATIONS: Tincture fresh aerial parts or roots 1:2 in 75 percent alcohol or dried aerial parts or roots 1:5. Standard tea or oil infusion. Leaf or root macerated for spit poultice to apply directly to external wounds, bites, or toothache.

SAFETY CONSIDERATIONS: Generally regarded as safe.

DOSAGE: Take 30 to 100 drops tincture 3 times a day or 1 to 2 cups of tea daily. Oil massaged into lymph nodes or breast for mastitis.

PRESERVATION: Chop the flower and seed heads for drying. Dry the leaves whole. Wash and chop the roots for drying.

TIP: *There are several species of echinacea. This plant is on the United Plant Savers "at-risk" list, so do not harvest it from the wild. This shouldn't be a problem, since this plant is easily grown in the garden. Look for the species that is native to your area and grow it in your garden.*

ELDERBERRY

Sambucus nigra, S. canadensis

PARTS USED: Berry, flower, leaf

USES: Elderberry is an immunomodulator that helps combat colds, influenza, and lung congestion. Relieves constipation, reduces fever blisters, eases chicken pox, breaks up mucus, and soothes a sore throat. Elderflower helps cool down the body during summer heat and fevers; increases the flow of urine; removes built-up uric acid to reduce inflammation of gout, arthritis, rheumatism, cardiovascular disease, diabetes, metabolic syndrome, and uric acid stone formation; and tones the face. Applied externally to heal wounds, cuts, and burns.

GROWING: Elder is a perennial shrub growing to a height of 25 feet and is found at the edges of woodland in part shade to full sun. Elder likes damp conditions, and is often found growing in drainage ditches near agricultural crops and will tolerate a variety of soils. Elderberries grow rather quickly and will need little care other than to weed as they are becoming established. Harvest the flowers right as they begin to bloom. Harvest the berries when the majority of them have turned deep purple.

PREPARATIONS: Tincture fresh berries 1:1 in 75 percent alcohol or dried berries 1:5. Make into a standard tea or syrup.

SAFETY CONSIDERATIONS: Generally regarded as safe. Use with caution if dehydrated as Elderberry is a diuretic and can further deplete fluids from the body. Berries should be cooked before eating to avoid their laxative effect. Root and bark can cause extreme vomiting. Avoid red-berried species as many are toxic.

DOSAGE: Take 30 drops tincture 3 times a day or every 2 hours for an acute situation. Drink 1 to 2 cups of tea daily. Take 1 tablespoon syrup as needed.

PRESERVATION: Destem the berries and dry or freeze on a cookie sheet for future use. The leaves can be harvested in the spring for drying. The flowers can be dried on a silicone mat.

TIP: *Use a fork to easily remove the berries from the stem when harvesting the berries.*

FENNEL

Foeniculum vulgare, F. vulgare azoricum

PARTS USED: Seed, bulb, leaf, stalk

USES: Used mainly as a digestive herb for reducing gas, bloating, constipation, and spasms. Soothes inflamed, irritated eyes; may reduce cataracts; eases menstrual cramping; reduces nausea and morning sickness; increases milk supply; reduces spasmodic congested coughs; breaks up thick, stuck mucus, especially in cases of bronchitis, congestion, asthma, and emphysema; eases shortness of breath, hoarseness, coughs, and congestion; and increases flow of urine to decrease water retention.

GROWING: Fennel is a perennial that grows to a height of 8 feet. Prefers full sun to part shade in well-drained soil and is drought tolerant once established. Fennel does not like transplanting; so if growing from seed, sow directly or plant in a compostable pot that can be directly planted. Apply Comfrey Fertilizer (page 125) or compost once a year in the early spring. Trim off dead growth at the end of the growing season. Harvest seeds once they turn brown on the stalk. Harvest leaves and stalks during growing season. Harvest bulbs in late summer or fall.

PREPARATIONS: Tincture seeds 1:4 in 60 percent alcohol. Make into a standard tea.

SAFETY CONSIDERATIONS: Generally regarded as safe, though large doses can overstimulate the nervous system and pregnant women should avoid therapeutic doses.

DOSAGE: Take 30 to 60 drops tincture 2 to 3 times a day or 1 to 2 cups of tea daily.

PRESERVATION: Dry the seeds on a tray for use later. Fennel leaves and bulbs can be chopped up and added to ice cubes with a bit of olive oil or water and frozen.

TIP: *Fennel is a preferred food of swallowtail caterpillars. Grow some in your garden to encourage the butterflies in your garden.*

GARLIC

Allium sativum

PARTS USED: Clove

USES: Effective against antibiotic-resistant diseases and fungal parasites, ringworm, and candida. Reduces fever; flushes the kidneys; thins mucus; expels bile from the gallbladder and liver; strengthens the heart and blood vessels; lowers blood pressure and cholesterol; boosts the immune system; clears urinary tract infections; reduces respiratory infections, including pneumonia, colds, asthma, and bronchitis; eases allergies; effective against earaches and ear infections, pertussis, tuberculosis, hypoglycemia, diabetes, arthritis, cancer, and atherosclerosis; and removes toxins from heavy metal poisoning.

GROWING: Garlic is a garden annual, best planted in the fall for a harvest the following summer. Apply Comfrey Fertilizer (page 125) or compost to encourage growth. Plant about 4 inches apart in a raised garden bed or garden row. Garlic tolerates a variety of soils as long as they are well drained. Weed in the spring and mulch heavily with straw or grass clippings to reduce weeds from growing up between them. Harvest in the summer, generally in the beginning of July, once the tops die back. Brush off the soil, place in the shade for a few days to dry, then store in a paper sack in a cool, dark place.

PREPARATIONS: For antibiotic or antibacterial qualities, add raw to food before serving. Cooked garlic still offers blood-pressure- and cholesterol-lowering benefits. See Pickled Garlic recipe (page 80) for another great way to consume garlic raw. Tincture bulbs 1:4 in 60 percent alcohol. Standard tea or oil infusion.

SAFETY CONSIDERATIONS: Generally regarded as safe.

DOSAGE: Take 30 drops tincture 3 times a day or 1 to 2 cups of tea daily. For ear infections (do not use if a perforated eardrum is suspected), use 5 to 10 drops of infused oil. Include 2 to 3 cloves of garlic in food daily.

PRESERVATION: Dry bulbs to use whole or dehydrate and powder.

TIP: *If your garlic develops scapes (flowering parts), trim them off before blooming to force the bulb to grow bigger. The scapes can be sautéed in butter for serving on top of your meals for a subtle garlicky flavor.*

LAVENDER

Lavandula angustifolia

PARTS USED: Flower, leaf

USES: Prevents infections; cleans; disinfects; eases pain; promotes healing in wounds; soothes burns and sunburns; reduces inflammation; eases stress- and anxiety-based headaches; stimulates the appetite; increases digestion; soothes insect bites and stings; reduces insomnia; reduces agitation in dementia patients; and eases heart palpitations, anxiety, and panic attacks.

GROWING: Lavender is a tender perennial from the Mediterranean that grows to a height of 3 feet. Lavender prefers a more arid climate and is fairly drought tolerant once established, adapting well to a variety of soils. Plant in full sun and mulch heavily to cut down on weeds since lavender grows enough to shade out other plants. Apply Comfrey Fertilizer (page 125) or compost once a year in the early spring. Harvest the flowers as soon as the spikes begin to open, cutting away spikes from the plant. Leaves can be harvested throughout the growing season.

PREPARATIONS: Tincture fresh flowers or leaves 1:2 in 65 percent alcohol or dried flowers or leaves 1:5. Make a standard tea or oil infusion. Macerate the leaf or flower for a spit poultice to apply directly to external wounds, bites, burns.

SAFETY CONSIDERATIONS: Generally regarded as safe.

DOSAGE: Take 30 drops tincture 3 times a day or 1 to 2 cups of tea daily.

PRESERVATION: Dry on trays, then store in a cool, dark place.

TIP: *If you live in a colder climate, prune back your plants heavily in the autumn, then mulch with straw or leaves to insulate against the freezing temperature.*

MARSHMALLOW

Althaea officinalis

PARTS USED: Root, leaf, flower

USES: Soothes hot, dry coughs from bronchitis, pertussis, and other respiratory ailments. Eases digestive issues and inflamed bladders; soothes the stomach, intestines, and esophagus lining caused by ulcers, acid reflux, and inflammation of the gut; heals wounds internally and externally; relieves toothaches; soothes and reduces canker sores, ulcers, cuts, bites, inflamed gums, and sore throats; relieves constipation; stimulates the flow of milk; relieves mastitis, wounds, bruises, cuts, mild burns, sunburns, and psoriasis; and soothes inflamed, dry, and irritated eyes.

GROWING: Marshmallow is a perennial that grows to 6 feet and prefers full sun. Place in the back of your garden area to reduce blocking out the sun of the plants growing around it. Marshmallow likes swampy conditions but can tolerate drought once established. Roots are a taproot and grow fairly deeply, so plant where you want this plant to remain. Marshmallow grows well in a variety of soils but prefers soil that holds moisture, such as clay. Apply Comfrey Fertilizer (page 125) or compost once a year in the early spring. Harvest leaves in spring and summer, lying flat to dry. Harvest flowers as they bloom for drying. Roots should be dug in early spring or late fall after the upper growth has begun to die back. Crowns can be removed and replanted to continue their growth.

PREPARATIONS: Tincture fresh roots 1:2 in 65 percent alcohol or dried root 1:5. Infusion of roots should be made with lukewarm to cool water to avoid the "slime factor." Try leaves instead for less slime if it's too thick to consume. Make a standard tea with leaf or flower. Leaf poultice applied to breasts for mastitis, inflammation, ulcers, wounds, and so on.

SAFETY CONSIDERATIONS: Generally regarded as safe.

DOSAGE: Take 15 to 30 drops tincture 3 times a day or 1 to 2 cups of tea or infusion daily.

PRESERVATION: Wash the roots well. Chop, then dry them on trays or in a dehydrator. Lie leaves or flowers flat to dry.

TIP: *In a pinch, flowers and leaves of okra, hollyhock, and rose of Sharon can be used similarly to marshmallow.*

MULLEIN

Verbascum thapsus

PARTS USED: Flower, leaf, root

USES: Leaf can be applied externally for sunburn, tumors, ulcers, hemorrhoids, swollen lymph, and varicosities. Leaf can also be used in smoking blends for hacking coughs, asthma, and spasmodic coughs. Flowers infused in oil soothes inner ear ailments, hemorrhoids, varicosities, as well as gum and mouth ulcers. Roots ease lower back complaints, lymph issues, and urinary incontinence. Realigns broken bones and slipped discs and lubricates the spinal cord.

GROWING: Mullein is a biennial plant growing to a height of 8 feet. This plant tolerates hot, dry conditions and is often found growing alongside ditches, railroad tracks, and waste areas. It prefers full sun and well-drained soil and once established needs low amounts of water. Mullein is easy to grow and establish, and its big leaves shade out other plants nearby, keeping the area around it weed free. Apply Comfrey Fertilizer (page 125) or compost once a year in the early spring. Harvest the roots between the autumn of the first year and the spring of the second year. Harvest the flowers as they appear on the stalks. Harvest leaves in the first year or at the beginning of the second year before the flower stalk appears.

PREPARATIONS: Tincture fresh roots 1:2 in 65 percent alcohol or dried root 1:5. Tincture fresh leaf 1:2 in 50 percent alcohol or dried leaf 1:5 in 25 percent alcohol. Make a standard infusion of the flower in oil or the leaf in a tea or infusion.

SAFETY CONSIDERATIONS: Generally regarded as safe. Strain leaf infusions to avoid irritation from fine hairs. Seeds are mildly toxic and should not be used. Leaf contains coumarin, so use with caution if taking a blood thinner. Do not use ear oil if a ruptured eardrum is suspected.

DOSAGE: Take 20 to 30 drops tincture up to 4 times a day or 1 to 2 cups of tea daily. Use 5 to 6 drops of warmed oil in each ear for earaches or built-up earwax.

PRESERVATION: Place the flowers in olive oil as they bloom. Lay the leaves flat and dry them on a screen. Mullein roots should be washed and chopped, then dried on a screen.

TIP: *Use a coffee filter or cloth Gerber baby diaper to strain out fine hairs from tea or tincture to avoid any irritations from the hairs.*

ONICN

Allium cepa

PARTS USED: Bulb

USES: When eaten raw, onion prevents growth of *Helicobacter pylori,* which can cause ulcers. Can be applied externally as a poultice or plaster to wounds and sores. Draws out pus and infection, soothes inflammation, and calms lung spasms. Internally, tincture can help with chronic bladder infections. Stimulates the circulatory system to reduce angina, arteriosclerosis, and heart attacks, and eases coughs, colds, and flu.

GROWING: Plant onions in early spring in rows 4 to 6 inches apart by planting sets, root-side down, about 1 inch beneath the surface. Compost the soil well and water it well. If starting with seeds, start indoors either in the autumn or midwinter, as onions are a biennial and need a long growing season to grow a decent bulb. Weed thoroughly and mulch with grass clippings to avoid weeds choking out baby onions. Onions grown from sets can be harvested throughout the season, using early growth as scallions, then using the bulb further in the season once it matures. Harvest in late summer or early fall, brushing off the soil and allowing them to cure in the shade for several days.

PREPARATIONS: Tincture fresh onion 1:2 in 65 percent alcohol or dried onion 1:5. Place raw onion slice externally on wounds, or make a plaster by sautéing a sliced onion with a bit of flour, then placing a piece of flannel on the chest to help draw out phlegm and ease coughing spasms. Make a standard syrup of onion to ease coughs.

SAFETY CONSIDERATIONS: Generally regarded as safe.

DOSAGE: Take 10 to 30 drops tincture 3 times a day or 1 to 2 cups of tea daily. Apply plaster daily as needed to help expectorate phlegm and reduce coughing. Take 1 to 3 teaspoons syrup to ease coughs.

PRESERVATION: Place cured onions in a dark, cool location.

TIP: *Onion's antibacterial properties go away when cooked, so if you are using the onion as an antibacterial, use it raw.*

PEACH

Prunus persica

PARTS USED: Leaf, bark, flower

USES: Soothes insect stings and inflammation, including digestive inflammation. Calms coughs from pertussis and other respiratory ailments, including dry, tickling coughs. Stops nervous twitches and spasms, eases nausea and vomiting, reduces diarrhea, calms immune system during allergic and asthmatic episodes, reduces anxiety and tension, reduces feelings of burnout and insomnia, and expels intestinal worms.

GROWING: Peach trees are a deciduous tree growing to 23 feet in height. Plant in the orchard 12 to 15 feet apart from other trees or along the edge of your property in full sun. Mulch heavily around the base and water often until the roots are established. Apply Comfrey Fertilizer (page 125) or compost once a year in the early spring. Harvest twigs in the spring when flowering, and collect the twigs, leaves, and flowers for making tinctures or drying.

PREPARATIONS: Tincture fresh leaf, flower, twig, or bark 1:2 in 65 percent alcohol or dried leaf, flower, twig, or bark 1:5. Apply compress of tincture to insect sting to reduce heat and swelling. Make into a standard tea or infused oil.

SAFETY CONSIDERATIONS: Generally regarded as safe.

DOSAGE: Take 30 drops tincture 3 times a day or every 20 minutes for an acute episode (such as an insect sting) or 1 to 2 cups of tea daily. Increase up to 4 cups daily to expel worms. Apply compress of leaf tincture to insect stings and inflammation. Apply oil externally to inflammation and insect stings as needed.

PRESERVATION: The twigs, inner bark, flower, and leaf can be dried on a screen.

TIP: *To sweeten your tincture, add a few slices of ripe peach when you make it.*

PEPPERMINT

Mentha x piperita

PARTS USED: Aerial parts during flowering

USES: Peppermint helps with a variety of chronic and acute digestive issues, including irritable bowel syndrome, diverticulitis, nausea, cramping, and poor digestion. Peppermint relieves menstrual cramping, eases tension and digestive headaches, relieves the pain of rheumatism and neuralgia, calms toothaches, reduces cavities, and heals other mouth inflictions, including gum issues. Peppermint cools from the inside out, helping lower fevers and cool the body during summer heat. Peppermint repels mice, rats, voles, and spiders.

GROWING: A perennial plant that grows to a height of about 2 feet. Prefers full sun, damp soil, and a fair amount of water. Can tolerate less water once established. Weed weekly until plants are well established, mulch then weed as needed. Apply Comfrey Fertilizer (page 125) or compost once a year in the early spring. Pinch back leaves heavily as the plant starts to flower to encourage bushy growth, and harvest as needed. Medicinally, peppermint is generally harvested during flowering.

PREPARATIONS: Tincture fresh 1:2 or dried 1:4 in 65 percent alcohol. Drink 1 to 2 cups of tea as needed. Add 60 drops of tincture in 2 tablespoons water for a mouthwash.

SAFETY CONSIDERATIONS: Generally regarded as safe.

DOSAGE: Take 30 to 60 drops of tincture 3 to 5 times a day or 1 to 2 cups of tea as needed. Use as mouthwash 2 to 3 times daily.

PRESERVATION: Dry on the stem, then strip off the leaf for storage.

TIP: *If you find peppermint to be too strong, try using spearmint instead, which is a milder mint with the same properties.*

RASPBERRY

Rubus occidentalis, R. idaeus

PARTS USED: Leaf, root, fruit

USES: Uterine tonic that aids in reproductive health in both men and women. Eliminates or reduces hormonal migraines and reduces diarrhea. Lowers fevers, reduces high blood pressure, improves cholesterol, reduces blood sugar issues, and eases nausea. Applied externally it disinfects wounds, reduces scarring, and tones the skin.

GROWING: Raspberry grows well on the edge of your garden, preferring full sun to part shade and has a tendency to become dense, making a good barrier. Raspberry is a perennial that grows biennial canes or stems; in the first year, it produces only leaves, whereas in the second year, it bears flowers and fruits. The cane tips will root and start new plants, an easy way to propagate more plants. Plant raspberry plants 8 to 12 inches apart and mulch heavily. Apply Comfrey Fertilizer (page 125) or compost once a year in the early spring. Raspberries grow well in a variety of soils and prefer a fair amount of moisture. Water well daily to help establish their roots, then water 1 to 2 times a week. Once they are established, they will not need supplemental water. Harvest roots in the spring, which will also help control the excess growth habit. Harvest leaves in the spring before flowers appear. Harvest fruits in the summer as they ripen.

PREPARATIONS: Tincture of fresh leaf 1:2 in 40 percent alcohol or dried leaf 1:4 in 60 percent alcohol. Roots can be chopped and tinctured 1:2 in 40 percent alcohol or made into a standard syrup. Leaf can be made as a standard tea or infusion.

SAFETY CONSIDERATIONS: Generally regarded as safe. Nursing mothers should not use excessive amounts, as it can dry up breast milk.

DOSAGE: Take 30 drops root tincture or 1 to 3 teaspoons syrup every 20 minutes for diarrhea. Take 30 to 60 drops leaf tincture 4 to 6 times a day. Drink 1 to 2 cups of tea daily.

PRESERVATION: Dry the leaves on a screen. Wash the roots well, then chop and dry. The berries can be dehydrated or frozen to use later.

TIP: *Raspberries can be switched with other Rubus species such as blackberry and wineberry.*

ROSE

Rosa rugosa, R. virginiana, R. canina

PARTS USED: Flower, hip

USES: Rose petals assist with lowering blood pressure and increasing circulation. Relieves diarrhea, mouth sores, and ulcers; reduces inflammation; eases urinary inflammation, IBS, constipation, and yeast and vaginal infections; soothes sore throats; and regulates menstrual cycles. Apply externally as a poultice to wounds and sore, irritated eyes.

GROWING: Rose is a woody perennial shrub that prefers moist conditions and can grow in full sun to partial shade. Roses can be started from seeds by collecting them from the rose hips and scattering the seeds in a container. Let them sit outdoors throughout the winter, and in the spring, seedlings should start to appear. They can then be separated and planted in individual pots to continue their growth until they are big enough to plant out in your garden. Plant on the edges of your garden to provide a barricade and mulch heavily. Apply Comfrey Fertilizer (page 125) or compost once a year in the early spring. If your soil is heavy with clay, add some limestone to help reduce the soil acidity. To increase the acidity, add coffee grounds around the bushes. Harvest petals right after flowers open. If you want to collect hips later in the season, pull the petals off the bush, leaving the reproductive parts intact, and hips will continue to form. Harvest hips after the first frost of the year. Avoid hybridized roses, as they lack medicinal value; instead look for species such as *Rosa rugosa, R. virginia,* and *R. canina.*

PREPARATIONS: Tincture petals fresh 1:2 or dried 1:5 in 65 percent alcohol or make a standard tea. Use rose hips in a standard infusion. Use petals or hips 1:2 in honey or standard syrup.

SAFETY CONSIDERATIONS: Generally regarded as safe.

DOSAGE: Take 15 to 30 drops tincture 3 times a day or 1 to 2 cups of tea or infusion daily. Take 1 to 3 teaspoons honey or syrup as needed for sore throats.

PRESERVATION: Dry the petals and hips on screens, then store in a cool, dark location.

TIP: *Rose hips contain fine hairs, so if you are using them for tea, use a coffee filter or cloth Gerber baby diaper to strain your tea.*

SAGE

Salvia officinalis

PARTS USED: Leaf, flower

USES: Helps reduce, suppress, and prevent excessive perspiration, and reduces the levels of expressed fluids in the body, including breast milk, saliva, and perspiration. Stimulates the uterus and brings on delayed menses; stimulates the production of bile flow; stimulates digestion; stimulates the hormones and the circulatory system, which can affect and enhance memory function; reduces hot flashes; boosts natural estrogen production; improves liver function; and relaxes peripheral blood vessels to increase blood flow through the skin and tissues while decreasing blood pressure. Eases sore throats, laryngitis, pharyngitis, tonsillitis, mouth ulcers, and gum disease.

GROWING: Sage is a semiwoody tender perennial that grows to 24 inches in height. Sage is a plant from the Mediterranean and loves a sunny spot in the garden in well-drained, somewhat dry soil and can tolerate a variety of soils, including clay, sand, and loam, as long as these conditions are met. Mulch heavily, weed weekly, and water daily until the plant becomes established, then water weekly during dry periods. Apply Comfrey Fertilizer (page 125) or compost once a year in the early spring. To harvest, use kitchen shears to snip off sprigs as needed. Sage leaves can be harvested all throughout the growing season, even when in flower. Harvest sage blossoms in the spring before they open.

PREPARATIONS: Tincture fresh 1:2 or dried 1:5 in 65 percent alcohol or make a standard tea.

SAFETY CONSIDERATIONS: Generally regarded as safe, though contains thujone and should be avoided in therapeutic doses by epileptics.

DOSAGE: Take 30 to 60 drops tincture 3 times a day or 1 to 2 cups of tea daily. Gargle with tea for a sore throat.

PRESERVATION: Dry on the stem, then strip off the leaf for storage. If you prefer to harvest only the leaves without stems, you can dry them singly on a mesh drying tray.

TIP: *If you have trouble keeping sage alive throughout the winter, surround it with a tomato cage; mulch heavily with straw, leaves, or grass clippings; and wrap in plastic.*

STINGING NETTLES

Urtica dioica

PARTS USED: Leaf, seed, root

USES: Reduces arthritic pain and increases circulation (direct contact with stingers); restores lung tissue; decreases anemia; nourishing to the body; desensitizes against allergens; breaks down allergen proteins; increases flow of milk; flushes the kidneys and bladder; dissolves urinary stones, gallstones, and gravel; cleanses the kidneys and liver; and increases kidney function. The root is specific for prostate issues.

GROWING: Nettles are perennials that grow to a height of 3 to 8 feet, preferring to grow in part shade to full sun and are often found at the edge of the woods or within the woods in a clearing. Nettles grow in just about any kind of soil and once established do not need weeding. Harvest the roots (rhizomes or stolons) in the spring or fall. Harvest the leaves in the spring before the plant flowers, or continually harvest throughout the growing season by cutting to the first set of leaves. Harvest seeds after flowering while they are still green. To harvest any part of this plant, you may want to wear gloves to avoid the stingers.

PREPARATIONS: Parts tinctured separately. Tincture fresh leaf or root 1:2 in 75 percent alcohol or dried plant or seed 1:5 in 50 percent alcohol. Make a standard infusion of the leaves.

SAFETY CONSIDERATIONS: Generally regarded as safe, though harvest with caution as nettles have stingers. Avoid harvesting the leaf once the plant starts to flower, as the buildup of formic acid in the leaves may irritate the kidneys.

DOSAGE: Take 30 to 60 drops of any tincture 3 to 4 times daily. Drink 1 to 2 cups leaf infusion daily.

PRESERVATION: Dry on the stem, then strip off the leaf for storage. Dry the seeds on a silicone screen. Wash the roots and rhizomes well, then chop and dry.

TIP: *Some species of nettles have a stronger sting than others. Nettle stingers dissipate when the plant is dried or cooked.*

THYME

Thymus vulgaris

PARTS USED: Flowering tops

USES: Used for respiratory issues, including pertussis, bronchitis, colds, influenza, and pneumonia, when presented with wet, spasmodic coughs. Soothes sore throats; clears up mucus and congestion; eases colic, gas, and bloating; and expels roundworms and flatworms.

GROWING: Thyme is a semiwoody perennial that grows 6 to 8 inches in height and is a bit sprawling. Thyme is a plant from the Mediterranean and loves a sunny spot in the garden in well-drained, somewhat dry soil and can tolerate a variety of soils, including clay, sand, and loam, as long as these conditions are met. Weed weekly and water daily until the plant becomes established, then water weekly during dry periods. Apply Comfrey Fertilizer (page 125) or compost once a year in the early spring. Once thyme is established, little weeding is generally needed as it grows thickly. To harvest, use kitchen shears to snip off sprigs as needed. Thyme can be harvested all throughout the growing season, even when in flower.

PREPARATIONS: Tincture fresh 1:2 or dried 1:4 in 65 percent alcohol or make a standard tea.

SAFETY CONSIDERATIONS: Generally regarded as safe.

DOSAGE: Take 30 drops tincture 3 times a day or 1 to 2 cups of tea daily.

PRESERVATION: Dry on the stem, then strip off the leaf for storage.

TIP: *Thyme is an excellent wormer for both humans and animals and can be used alone or with other herbs as a tincture or tea.*

WILLOW

Salix spp.

PARTS USED: Leaf, twig, inner bark

USES: Used to ease aches and pains, muscle spasms, inflammation, rheumatism, arthritis, gout, back pain, headaches, and neuralgia. Helps reduce stomachaches, helps lower fevers and relieves nervous insomnia.

GROWING: Willow is a dioecious, deciduous tree, growing up to 70 feet. Willow prefers to grow in places where its roots have continuous access to water, so it is often found growing near streams, riverbanks, ponds, lakes, and other bodies of fresh water or in low-lying areas where water pools after rain. Willow needs a fair amount of sunlight and grows well on the edge of property or near any water source you might have available. Young trees should be watered weekly during droughts and once established will not need further watering. Willow tolerates most soils, tends to grow rapidly, and will hybridize easily with any other species of willow growing nearby. Harvest the leaves in spring and summer and the inner bark or twigs in spring or fall when the sap is rising or falling.

PREPARATIONS: Tincture leaf, inner bark, or twig fresh 1:2 in 60 percent alcohol or dried 1:4 in 40 percent alcohol, or make into a standard oil. All parts can be made into a standard tea.

SAFETY CONSIDERATIONS: Use with caution if pregnant. Those on blood thinners or with hemophilia should avoid willow. Do not give to children with a viral infection with headaches. Use with caution if you are allergic to aspirin.

DOSAGE: Take 30 drops tincture 3 times daily. Apply the oil to arthritis, achy muscles, or sprained muscles 2 to 3 times daily. Drink 1 cup of tea 3 times daily, sweetening if desired.

PRESERVATION: Dry the leaves, twigs, and bark on screens.

TIP: *Twigs are easier to harvest than inner bark and harvesting them reduces the risk of damaging the tree. They can be easily stripped using a knife by scraping down the length of the twig. For thin twigs less than ¼ inch in diameter, chop into small pieces without stripping.*

||||||||||||||||||||||||||||||||||||||||

CHAPTER FIVE

RECIPES FOR EATING

BASIL-INFUSED OIL

MAKES 1 CUP

This oil is a great way to preserve the flavor of basil for use throughout the year! It mixes well with an infused vinegar to make salad dressing, and can be drizzled over steamed vegetables for a punch of flavor. Medicinally, it can be used as a massage oil for tired, sore muscles or to soothe dry, itchy skin.

½ cup recently dried basil

1 cup olive oil

Follow the instructions in chapter 3 for making an herb-infused oil (page 21) using the basil and olive oil.

TO USE: Combine equal amounts of an infused oil and an infused vinegar, such as basil, garlic, sage blossom, or dandelion, to make a salad dressing. Drizzle over vegetables. Massage into achy muscles.

VARIATIONS: Infused oils can be made with a variety of herbs. Try combining other herbs with the basil for a more rounded flavor. Thyme, rosemary, sage, and garlic are all great additions as long as you keep the ½-cup-to-1-cup ratio of dried herbs to oil.

STORAGE: Store Basil-Infused Oil in an airtight jar in the refrigerator and use within 1 year.

CANDIED MINT LEAVES

MAKES 36 CANDIED LEAVES

Not only are these a great after-dinner breath freshener, but they also help settle the stomach when you've had too much to eat or are feeling nauseous. And they are perfect anytime you just want a little refreshing treat.

1 egg white

1 cup granulated sugar

36 dry fresh mint leaves, stemmed

1. Preheat the oven to 225°F. Line a baking sheet with parchment paper.

2. In a small bowl, whisk the egg white until it is bubbly.

3. Put the sugar in a separate small bowl.

4. Dip the mint leaves one by one in the egg white, then in the sugar.

5. Place the coated leaves on the lined baking sheet, making sure the leaves don't touch.

6. Bake for 20 to 30 minutes, turning the leaves every 10 minutes, or until the leaves are completely dry.

7. Once they are dry, remove from the oven, and allow them to cool.

8. Place in an airtight jar between layers of parchment paper.

TO USE: Eat one as desired for a breath freshener or 1 to 2 for a stomach soother. Use them to decorate cupcakes or add a leaf to a cup of tea for a minty splash of flavor.

VARIATIONS: Try this with lemon balm or violet flowers. The lemony taste of the lemon balm is amazing, and candied violet flowers add a lovely decorative touch to cupcakes.

STORAGE: Store in a cool, dry location and use within a week.

CHAI HONEY

MAKES 16 OUNCES

This flavorful and healing honey can be used to flavor an ordinary cup of tea or taken by the spoonful to soothe a sore throat.

3 tablespoons fennel seeds

1 tablespoon dried
   ginger roots

½ tablespoon crushed
   cardamom pods

½ tablespoon whole cloves

¾ teaspoon peppercorns

6 crumbled bay leaves

3 crushed cinnamon sticks

16 ounces raw honey

1. In a 16-ounce mason jar, combine the fennel seeds, ginger, cardamom, cloves, peppercorns, bay leaves, and cinnamon.

2. Gently heat the honey over medium-low heat. Do not let it boil. (You only need to warm it to thin it a bit.)

3. Pour the honey into the jar over the herbs, use a chopstick or butter knife to stir, then cover with an airtight lid.

4. Let steep for 2 to 4 weeks, turning daily to keep the herbs well mixed with the honey.

5. Pour the honey into a medium saucepan and warm gently again to thin.

6. Strain the honey through a cheesecloth to remove the herbs.

7. Compost the herbs and cap the honey jar.

TO USE: Add 1 to 3 teaspoons of infused honey to a cup of tea. For a sore throat, take 1 teaspoon as needed or add 1 teaspoon of honey to 1 cup of hot water with the juice of ½ lemon.

VARIATIONS: Or add dried, roasted dandelion or burdock root to give the honey a more earthy flavor.

STORAGE: Store in an airtight jar in a cool, dark location, and your infused honey will last for several years.

DEEP ROOTS DRINK
(A COFFEE SUBSTITUTE)

SERVES 17 TO 26

Trying to give up coffee? This blend is dark and nourishing and makes for a great substitute! The secret is in the roasting.

1 cup dried burdock roots

1 cup dried dandelion roots

1 cup dried chicory roots

¼ cup dried
  marshmallow roots

1. Preheat the oven to 225°F.

2. Spread out the burdock, dandelion, chicory, and marshmallow roots on a baking sheet and put them in the oven.

3. Roast for 20 to 30 minutes, stirring every 5 to 10 minutes.

4. When the roots are a rich brown color and smell aromatic, they are ready to be removed.

5. Remove from the oven and allow to cool.

6. Stir to mix, then pour into an airtight jar.

TO USE: Put 2 to 3 tablespoons of roasted roots in a saucepan. Add 16 ounces filtered water, bring to a boil over medium-high heat, then reduce the heat to medium-low and simmer for 15 to 20 minutes. Strain, reserving the liquid, and add honey—try the Chai Honey (page 68)—and cream to taste.

VARIATIONS: If you want an even stronger medicinal boost, after the roots have roasted and cooled, add 1 cup of crumbled reishi or turkey tail mushrooms.

STORAGE: Store in a cool, dark location and use within 1 year.

ELDERBERRY DUMPLINGS
SERVES 9

This is a delicious dessert that goes great with homemade ice cream or fresh whipped cream.

2 cups fresh or frozen elderberries

⅔ cup raw honey

1 tablespoon flour, plus ¾ cup sifted

2 tablespoons freshly squeezed lemon juice

¾ cup water

1 teaspoon cream of tartar

½ teaspoon baking soda

½ teaspoon ground cinnamon

½ teaspoon sea salt

¼ cup sugar

¼ cup grated lemon zest

¼ cup milk

1 egg

1. Preheat the oven to 400°F.

2. In a medium saucepan, mix together the berries, honey, 1 tablespoon of flour, the lemon juice, and water. Gently warm the mixture over low heat.

3. While the mixture is heating, in a medium bowl, combine the remaining ¾ cup of flour, the cream of tartar, baking soda, cinnamon, salt, sugar, and lemon zest.

4. In a small bowl, combine the milk and egg, mixing well.

5. Pour the wet ingredients into the dry ingredients, stirring just enough to combine.

6. Once the berry mixture has thickened, pour it into an 8- or 9-inch square baking dish.

7. Drop spoonfuls of dumpling dough into the berry sauce.

8. Bake for 25 to 30 minutes, or until the dumplings are lightly browned. Remove from the oven.

TO USE: Serve with freshly whipped cream or vanilla ice cream.

VARIATIONS: Use only 1 cup elderberries and add 1 cup peaches or raspberries.

ELDERBERRY SYRUP

MAKES 4 CUPS

This syrup is extremely versatile. It can be used for fighting off colds and influenza or drizzled on pancakes or ice cream. It can be added to herbal teas for an extra boost of vitamin C, used to enhance the flavor of teas, or even made into a soda for a summertime refreshment.

2 cups elderberries

2 cups water

2 cups honey

1. In a medium saucepan, combine the elderberries and water and bring to boil over high heat.

2. Turn off the heat and mash the berries.

3. Cover and steep for 1 hour.

4. Strain the berries and return the infusion to the saucepan.

5. Add the honey and gently warm over low heat until the honey is thin and easily stirred into the elderberry infusion.

6. Allow to cool, then pour into a bottle and secure the cap.

TO USE: Add a teaspoon to herbal tea or drizzle on pancakes in place of syrup.

VARIATIONS: To make elderberry soda, add 2 ounces of syrup to every 8 ounces of seltzer water. Mix well.

STORAGE: Store syrup in the refrigerator for up to 4 months.

GREEN MAN PESTO

MAKES ABOUT 3½ CUPS

This pesto makes use of the natural abundance of nettles, basil, and walnuts while making a delicious topping that can be used with any pasta, including Nettles Pasta (page 77) or any other way you usually enjoy pesto. Be sure to handle uncooked nettles carefully, or wear gloves, as they can sting until they are cooked.

1 cup fresh stinging nettles

1 cup fresh basil

2 garlic cloves

½ cup olive oil

4 to 5 ounces
Parmesan cheese

3 to 4 ounces walnuts

Put the nettles, basil, garlic, oil, cheese, and walnuts in a food processor or blender, and blend until smooth. If it's too thick, add a bit more oil.

TO USE: Use as you would any other pesto. A few tablespoons can be stirred into pasta, or it can be spread on mini toasts, topped with a slice of tomato and mozzarella, and drizzled with olive oil.

VARIATIONS: Use an infused oil to add another layer of flavor to this pesto. You can replace the nettles with other weeds, such as dandelion, violet, and chickweed, or use a combination of all of them.

STORAGE: Store in the refrigerator and use within 2 weeks, or spoon into ice cube trays and freeze. Once frozen, transfer them to a glass jar to store in the freezer for up to 1 year.

HERBED BUTTER

MAKES 1 CUP

This butter is a great way to jazz up your food, toast, and tea or coffee. Already delicious, butter becomes extraordinary with just a few herbs and a few minutes.

8 tablespoons (1 stick) butter, ghee, or coconut oil

2 teaspoons powdered thyme

2 teaspoons powdered sage

½ teaspoon powdered garlic

½ teaspoon powdered lavender

1. Put the butter in a saucepan over low heat.

2. Once the butter has melted, remove it from the heat and pour it into a wide-mouthed 8-ounce jar.

3. Add the powdered thyme, sage, garlic, and lavender to the butter and mix well.

4. Every 20 minutes or so, stir again to recombine the herbs.

5. Once it has almost completely set up, stir once more.

6. Screw on the lid to the jar and let sit at room temperature for 2 weeks.

TO USE: Spread this butter on toast or a bagel for a quick snack, add it to your favorite pot roast, or put some on top of your vegetables.

VARIATIONS: If you prefer a sweet, spicy herbed butter that is more of a dessert butter, replace the herbs with the following spices: 2 teaspoons ground cinnamon, 1 teaspoon ground allspice, ½ teaspoon ground cloves, and ½ teaspoon ground ginger.

STORAGE: Store in the refrigerator and use within 6 months.

HOMEMADE MARSHMALLOWS

MAKES ABOUT 24 MARSHMALLOWS

The flavor of homemade marshmallows reminds me of the circus peanuts candy I used to get as a kid. When marshmallows were made from the root, they were used as a cough remedy for kids and are especially helpful for dry, irritated, tickly coughs.

2 egg whites

½ teaspoon vanilla extract

½ cup raw sugar

2 tablespoons powdered
  marshmallow roots

1. Preheat the oven to 275°F. Line a baking sheet with parchment paper.

2. In a large bowl, beat the egg whites until very foamy and not quite stiff.

3. Add the vanilla.

4. Slowly beat in the sugar, 1 teaspoon at a time.

5. Once all of the sugar has been added, stir in the marshmallow root powder.

6. Using a teaspoon, drop the mixture on to the lined baking sheet.

7. Bake for 1 hour.

8. Remove from the oven and let cool.

TO USE: Serve with a cup of cocoa or chai.

VARIATIONS: These marshmallows are great when dipped in melted dark chocolate. To make heart-shaped marshmallows, mash 6 raspberries and stir them in after you mix in the marshmallow root powder in step 5. When dropping onto the tray, drop two ½ teaspoons side by side, using your finger to form a heart shape.

STORAGE: Wrap in parchment paper and store in a sealed bag or jar in the refrigerator. Consume within 2 weeks.

HOMESTEAD SEASONING BLEND

MAKES 10 TABLESPOONS

This is a great all-purpose seasoning blend that adds pizzazz to ordinary meals. It's versatile and can be used to add flavor to a variety of meat dishes. It goes especially well with poultry and fish but tastes great on vegetables, too. The addition of nettle seeds makes it great for kidney support.

5 teaspoons powdered thyme

4 teaspoons powdered sage

4 teaspoons powdered tarragon

1 tablespoon powdered lavender

1 tablespoon nettle seeds

1 tablespoon powdered dried mushrooms, such as turkey tail, reishi, or maitake

2 teaspoons powdered onion

2 teaspoons powdered garlic

2 teaspoons celery seed

1 teaspoon powdered basil

1 teaspoon pepper

In a small bowl, combine the thyme, sage, tarragon, lavender, nettle seeds, mushrooms, onion, garlic, celery seed, basil, and pepper, then pour into a shaker bottle with a lid.

TO USE: Add a few tablespoons when you are cooking ground meat or chicken. Sprinkle on vegetables to season them after cooking.

VARIATIONS: Switch out some of the herbs to vary the flavor. Add in some powdered fennel seeds to give it a more Italian flavor.

STORAGE: Store in an airtight jar in your cabinet with your other seasonings.

IMMUNI-C DRINK

SERVES 8

This is a great drink to boost the immune system when you're feeling a bit run-down. Elderberries give a sweet berry flavor, while the rose hips add some tang. The ginger gives it a bit of zip.

8 cups filtered water

½ cup crushed rose hips

½ cup minced fresh ginger roots

1 cup fresh elderberries or ½ cup dried

1 cup honey

1. In a medium saucepan, combine the water, rose hips, and ginger and bring to a boil over high heat. Reduce the heat to low and simmer for 15 to 20 minutes.

2. Add the elderberries, mashing them if they are fresh, and simmer for an additional 5 minutes.

3. Remove from the heat and let cool.

4. Strain the herbs, reserving the liquid. Return the liquid to the saucepan and compost the herbs. Reheat the liquid over low heat, just enough to thin the honey.

5. Add the honey and stir.

6. Pour into a quart jar, screw on the lid, and chill.

TO USE: Serve chilled with a sprig of peppermint.

VARIATIONS: Freeze in ice pop containers for a cool summertime treat.

STORAGE: Store in the refrigerator and consume within 1 month.

NETTLES PASTA

SERVES 4 TO 6

Use this pasta in place of your usual pasta in any recipe. A simple meal can be made from this pasta topped with some Green Man Pesto (page 72). Be sure to handle uncooked nettles carefully, or wear gloves, as they can sting until they are cooked.

1¼ cups fresh chopped stinging nettles

3 eggs

2 cups flour, plus more for dusting

1. In a medium saucepan fitted with a vegetable steamer tray, steam the nettles over medium heat until they are well cooked and mushy, about 15 minutes. Remove from the heat.

2. Put the cooked nettles in a cheesecloth, wrap them up, then twist and squeeze until all excess liquid has drained away.

3. Put the nettles and eggs in a blender or food processor, cover, and process until smooth.

4. Pour the nettle mixture into a large bowl and add the flour. Mix thoroughly with a fork until a dough forms.

5. Lightly flour a clean work surface. Turn out the dough onto the floured surface and knead it for 5 minutes, or until smooth and elastic.

6. Cover and let stand for 30 minutes.

7. Roll the dough in a pasta machine according to the manufacturer's instructions, or use a rolling pin and roll out a handful of dough at a time.

8. Lay the rolled-out pasta sheets on a clean dish towel while you finish rolling the dough.

CONTINUED ▶

9. Use a fettuccine attachment on your pasta machine to cut the noodles, or place a pasta sheet on a cutting board and use a knife, pizza cutter, or pasta cutter to cut the pasta into thin strips.

10. Hang the cut pasta on a drying rack (I use my wooden clothes-drying rack) until you are ready to cook them. At this point, you can place it in a sealed bowl and store it in the refrigerator, or you can cook them.

TO USE: Fill a stockpot half full of water and add a pinch of sea salt. Bring the water to a boil, then add the pasta and cook for 4 to 5 minutes. Drain the pasta, then add butter or oil to coat, stirring to combine well. Add your favorite pasta toppings.

VARIATIONS: Make stuffed ravioli with the dough by cutting it into 2-inch-by-4-inch strips, placing 1 tablespoon of seasoned cooked ground beef in the middle of the top halves of the rectangles, then folding the pasta in half and crimping all the edges with a fork to seal. Boil for 6 to 8 minutes. Serve buttered, with pesto, or with a tomato sauce.

STORAGE: Fresh pasta will last about a week in the refrigerator or it can be dried completely and stored in an airtight container at room temperature for up to 2 years.

PEACH SHRUB

MAKES 32 CUPS

Shrubs are syrups made from fruit, herbs, honey or sugar, and vinegar. They are refreshing, healthy alternatives to soda. They are also great for stimulating the appetite, which will aid in digestion.

2 cups organic peaches, cut into chunks (about 3 to 4 peaches)

1 cup raw sugar or raw honey

½ teaspoon molasses

1 cup red-wine vinegar

½ cup peach leaves

¼ cup fresh cinnamon basil leaves or lemon verbena leaves

Seltzer water

1. In a quart jar, combine the peaches, sugar, and molasses. Stir and mash the peaches. Screw on the lid and set aside in a cool, dark place for 8 hours.

2. In a separate quart jar, mix together the red-wine vinegar, peach leaves, and cinnamon basil leaves. Screw on the lid and set aside with the first jar for 8 hours (or up to 24).

3. Once 8 hours have elapsed, pour the vinegar mixture onto the peaches and sugar. Mix well and replace the lid.

4. Return your jar to a cool, dark area and let sit for 1 week.

5. Strain the peaches, leaves, and basil, returning the liquid to the jar. Compost the fruit and leaves. Put the lid on the jar and refrigerate for 1 week, tasting daily. Once the vinegar flavor has mellowed, it is ready to use.

TO USE: Add 1 ounce shrub to every 6 ounces chilled seltzer water.

VARIATIONS: Experiment with using other fruits and their leaves, such as blackberries, raspberries, apricots, or pears.

STORAGE: Store in the refrigerator and use within 6 months.

PICKLED GARLIC

MAKES 16 OUNCES

This is a recipe I learned from herbalist Rosemary Gladstar. It's one of my favorite ways to boost the immune system. The garlic mellows as it ages, making them a tasty treat, but don't eat too many or your friends and family won't want to be in the same room with you! If pickling with the vinegar, the end result is a sweet and tangy mix, whereas using the tamari or coconut aminos gives a sweeter and saltier flavor. They are equally good, so make a jar of each.

Enough garlic cloves to fill a 16-ounce jar (15 to 20 heads garlic, depending on size)

8 thyme sprigs

2 sage leaves

8 to 12 ounces apple cider vinegar, tamari, or coconut aminos

8 ounces raw honey

1. Without nicking the garlic, peel them and fill the 16-ounce jar, leaving about 1 inch of headspace.

2. Nestle the thyme sprigs and sage leaves into the jar.

3. Pour in the vinegar to cover the garlic, leaving about ¼ inch of headspace, and screw on the lid. (You may have leftover vinegar, depending on the size and shape of the garlic.) If the lid is metal, place a piece of wax paper over the jar before screwing on the lid to keep the vinegar from corroding the lid. (Label your jar with the ingredients and the date you started it. You may also wish to add the finish date on the jar so you know when you can use it.)

4. Let steep for 6 weeks. (If you are using vinegar, the garlic may turn a copper green color, which is perfectly normal.)

5. After 6 weeks, pour off half of the liquid and top the jar off with the honey, stirring to combine. (The liquid you've poured off can be used in cooking.)

6. Let steep for another 6 weeks, shaking occasionally.

TO USE: Eat 1 or 2 cloves of pickled garlic a day to keep your immune system in good health and to reap the benefits of eating raw garlic.

VARIATIONS: Experiment with adding other herbs, such as sliced ginger, rosemary sprigs, or monarda flowers (such as bee balm) to vary the flavor.

STORAGE: Store the jar in a cool, dark location in your kitchen cabinet.

ROSE HIP JELLY

MAKES 6 CUPS

Rose hip jelly is a delicious way to get a daily dose of vitamin C. It can be used like any jelly, served on toast or English muffins, or try adding a spoonful to your tea to sweeten it and give it extra zing.

8 cups fresh rose hips

6 cups water

½ cup freshly squeezed lemon juice

1 package liquid pectin

¼ teaspoon butter

3½ cups sugar

1. Put the rose hips in a large stockpot, add the water, and bring to a boil over high heat. Reduce the heat to low, cover, and simmer for about 1 hour (sometimes longer), or until the rose hips are soft and easy to mash.

2. Using a potato masher, mash the rose hips into a rough puree. Set a strainer lined with cheesecloth over a large bowl. Transfer the rose hip mash to the strainer and let sit for 1 hour, then gather up the rose hips in the cheesecloth and squeeze, capturing all of the liquid in the bowl.

3. Measure the liquid. You should have 3 cups. If you have less, pour hot water through the rose hips in the cheesecloth-lined strainer to make 3 cups.

4. Rinse the stockpot so it's free of any chunks of rose hip mash, then return the juice to the stockpot. Add the lemon juice and pectin. Bring to a boil over high heat and add the sugar. Boil for 1 minute, then remove from the heat.

5. Pour into sterile 8-ounce jelly jars, leaving ¼ inch of headspace. Wipe the jar rims, adjust the lids, and screw on the rings. Place in a water bath canner for 5 minutes (or skip canning and store in the freezer for up to 1 year).

TO USE: Spread this jelly on toast, pancakes, or English muffins, or add a teaspoonful to your cup of tea.

VARIATIONS: This recipe can be doubled if you have a lot of rose hips.

STORAGE: Store in a dark, cool location for up to 1 year.

SAGE BLOSSOM VINEGAR

MAKES 16 OUNCES

This is one of my favorite herbal vinegars. The flavor sage blossoms lend to the vinegar is indescribable. They have a more delicate sage flavor, which balances well with the vinegar. Sage blooms in late spring or early summer once it has established in the garden. The blooms are profuse and can be easily harvested to make a divine-tasting vinegar that can be used as a sore throat gargle, a digestive aid, or flavoring for a salad dressing or a hearty bowl of ham and bean soup. For best results, pick the blooms before they open. There is no need to wash them unless you feel they are dusty. If so, then give them a quick rinse and pat dry with a cloth.

1 cup sage blossoms

16 ounces apple cider vinegar

1. Put the sage blossoms in a 16-ounce jar.

2. Add the vinegar to fill the jar and screw on the lid. If the lid is metal, place a piece of wax paper over the jar before attaching the lid to keep the vinegar from corroding the lid. (Label your jar with the ingredients and the date you started it. You may also wish to add the finish date on the jar so you know when you can use it.)

3. Let steep for 3 to 4 weeks. After that point, you may leave the blossoms in the vinegar, or you may strain the blossoms, returning the liquid to the jar and composting the blossoms.

TO USE: If you want to use this as a gargle, add 1 tablespoon of vinegar to ¼ cup of warm water and gargle as needed to help relieve a sore throat. For use as a digestive aid, add 2 to 3 teaspoons of the vinegar to 1 cup of water and drink about 20 minutes before a meal. Use in place of a regular vinegar in a salad dressing recipe or sprinkle over any foods you enjoy eating with vinegar. The blossoms can be eaten or added as a garnish, similar to pickles.

VARIATIONS: If you've missed the blossoming period, you can still make an herbal vinegar from the leaves of your sage plant. Simply substitute chopped leaves for the blossoms. The flavor will be slightly different but the vinegar still can be used in the same way.

STORAGE: Store the vinegar in a cool, dark location in your kitchen cabinet.

SAUERKRAUT

MAKES 1 GALLON

Sauerkraut is a great way to get a healthy dose of probiotics, which are great for a healthy digestive system. The addition of herbs can help boost the digestive properties and enhance the flavor.

1 head green cabbage

4 garlic cloves, minced

2 tablespoons fennel seeds

1 tablespoon dried thyme

Sea salt

1. Sterilize a gallon jar, either glass or ceramic, and set aside.

2. Shred the cabbage in a food processor or by hand with a knife or mandoline.

3. Transfer the cabbage to a large bowl, and mix it together with the garlic, fennel seeds, and thyme.

4. Begin layering the shredded cabbage mixture in the jar with the sea salt by placing about an inch of cabbage followed by a thin layer of salt.

5. Repeat until all the cabbage has been used.

6. Place a small dish or other flat object on top of the cabbage, then fill a 16-ounce mason jar with water, cap it, and place it on top of the dish. Cover the gallon jar with a clean tea towel.

7. Store the jar in a cool location away from direct sunlight.

8. After 24 hours, check the sauerkraut. There should be liquid forming in the gallon jar. Press down on the mason jar filled with water to keep the plate submerged under the sauerkraut liquid. If there's not enough liquid to do this, add a bit of filtered water.

9. Continue checking your sauerkraut daily to make sure it's fully submerged in liquid. If any scum forms at the top, skim it off.

10. After a week, the sauerkraut will have fermented enough to eat. Taste it and see if it's to your liking. You can continue to ferment it for up to 6 weeks, and you will notice the bubbles disappear. At that point, you can remove the dish and the mason jar filled with water, put a lid on your sauerkraut, and store it in the refrigerator.

TO USE: Sauerkraut is a great side dish or topping for a variety of foods, including salads, tacos, and roasted meats.

VARIATIONS: Try adding other herbs to change the flavor. Dried basil, sage, rosemary, dill, and caraway are all great choices. You can also use purple cabbage to make a pretty purple-colored sauerkraut.

STORAGE: Store in the refrigerator and consume within 6 months.

SPRINGTIME FRITTERS WITH DIPPING SAUCE

MAKES 10 FRITTERS

These are a springtime favorite at our house and the variations are endless. They are great as a bread replacement for sandwiches, too.

FOR THE FRITTERS

½ cup chopped dandelion, stinging nettles, violet, or chickweed leaves (or a combination)

½ cup dandelion flower petals, removed from their tops

½ minced red onion

¼ cup coconut flour

¼ cup almond flour

2 eggs, beaten

1 garlic clove, minced

¼ teaspoon sea salt

¼ teaspoon black pepper

Ghee, butter, or coconut oil, for greasing the pan

FOR THE DIPPING SAUCE

¼ cup mayonnaise

¼ cup coconut milk

1 tablespoon minced fresh dill, thyme, or rosemary (or a combination)

1 tablespoon minced red onion

1 garlic clove, minced

1 tablespoon herb vinegar

2 dandelion flower heads, petals only

TO MAKE THE FRITTERS

1. In a large bowl, mix together the chopped dandelion, dandelion flower petals, onion, coconut flour, almond flour, eggs, garlic, salt, and pepper.

2. Heat a skillet over medium heat until hot, then grease the pan.

3. Spoon ¼ cup of the batter into the skillet, and fry for 3 to 4 minutes on each side, or until cooked through.

4. Repeat until all the dough has been used.

TO MAKE THE DIPPING SAUCE

5. In a small bowl, whisk together the mayonnaise, coconut milk, dill, onion, garlic, vinegar, and dandelion flower heads.

TO USE: Serve warm with the dipping sauce or make a sandwich using the fritters as the bread.

VARIATIONS: Add other springtime flowers, such as violets, to the mix. Add lemon balm leaves for a bit of lemony flavor in the fritters or add chives for an extra oniony flavor.

STORAGE: Keep the fritters in an airtight container and the sauce in a covered jar for 7 to 10 days in the refrigerator.

STEAMED NETTLES

SERVES 4

This is one of my favorite ways to prepare nettles, taking advantage of all the nutritional value this plant has to offer. For an extra punch of nettle goodness, replace the plain vinegar with a nettle-infused vinegar (see vinegar tincture, page 19). Be sure to handle uncooked nettles carefully, or wear gloves, as they can sting until they are cooked.

8 ounces fresh stinging nettle tops

1 tablespoon bacon grease, olive oil, or coconut oil

2 garlic cloves, minced

1 tablespoon apple cider vinegar

Sea salt

1. Carefully, or wearing gloves to protect your hands from stings, chop the nettle tops.

2. In a medium skillet, heat the bacon grease over medium heat.

3. When the oil is hot, add the nettles. Cover and steam for 2 to 3 minutes.

4. Remove the lid and stir briefly. Replace the lid and cook for another minute. Remove from the heat.

5. Add the garlic on top, drizzle with vinegar, and add sea salt to taste.

TO USE: Serve as a side dish with your meal. This also tastes great on top of rice, couscous, or quinoa.

VARIATIONS: If you like bacon, sauté 6 chopped bacon slices, then use the existing grease (you may wish to drain some off) to cook the recipe.

THYME–SEA SALT BLEND

MAKES 1½ CUPS

This blend is great on just about everything, but it's especially good on fish and poultry.

3 tablespoons dried thyme

2 tablespoons coriander seeds

2 tablespoons cumin seeds

1 tablespoon fennel seeds

1 cup Himalayan pink sea salt

1. Heat a medium cast-iron skillet over high heat, and add the thyme, coriander, cumin, and fennel. Stir until toasted and fragrant.

2. Remove from the heat. Transfer to a bowl.

3. Mix in the salt.

4. Fill an empty salt grinder with the blend, storing the remainder in a jar.

TO USE: Grind and use as you would generally use salt to season your food.

VARIATIONS: Try this with other herbs, such as sage, rosemary, basil, or lemon thyme.

STORAGE: Store in a cool, dry location.

CHAPTER SIX

RECIPES FOR HEALING AND WELLNESS

ALLERGY RELIEF TEA

MAKES 3 CUPS LOOSE TEA (48 CUPS BREWED TEA)

This tea helps stop the reaction to allergens. It soothes itchy eyes; calms sneezing fits; relieves a scratchy, raw throat; and combats general malaise. This tea is great for all types of allergens, including pet dander, environmental allergens, and plant pollen.

1 cup dried stinging
   nettle leaves

½ cup dried peach leaves

½ cup dried plantain leaves

½ cup dried elderflower

¼ cup dried
   chamomile flowers

¼ cup dried
   ragweed leaves

In a small bowl, combine the nettle leaves, peach leaves, plantain leaves, elderflower, chamomile flowers, and ragweed leaves. Transfer to an airtight container, and label with the ingredients and instructions for use.

TO USE: Steep 1 tablespoon tea blend in 8 ounces boiling water for 15 to 20 minutes. Drink a cup every couple of hours as needed.

VARIATIONS: You can add 2 tablespoons peppermint leaves to the blend to enhance the flavor.

STORAGE: Store in a cool, dark location and use within 1 year.

BARN CAT BALM

MAKES 4 OUNCES

There are no tigers on the homestead, but this salve works similarly to the popular commercial Tiger Balm. This salve can be applied to sore, achy muscles and will help relieve their pain. It works on any type of muscle aches, including menstrual cramps, pulled or strained muscles, back pain, and sore post-garden-workout muscles.

2 tablespoons dried rosemary leaves

2 tablespoons dried peppermint leaves

1½ tablespoons dried willow bark

1½ tablespoons dried basil leaves

1 tablespoon dried mullein roots

1½ cups olive oil

1 vitamin E gelcap

1½ ounces beeswax

1. Follow the instructions in chapter 3 for making an herb-infused oil and a salve (page 21) using the rosemary, peppermint, willow bark, basil, mullein, olive oil, vitamin E gelcap, and beeswax.

2. Label your salve with the name, ingredient list, and date it was made.

TO USE: Apply a small amount of salve to affected muscles and massage into the area. Repeat as needed. You may find that applying heat can help increase the effect of the salve.

VARIATIONS: You can also make a bath tea out of this combination of herbs. It is great to soak in before you apply the balm. To make the tea, use 1 cup dried rosemary, 1 cup dried peppermint, ½ cup dried willow bark, ½ cup dried basil leaves, and ½ cup dried mullein root, steeped in 1 gallon boiling water for about 30 minutes, before straining and pouring the liquid into bath water. (Compost the herbs.)

STORAGE: Store in a cool, dark location and use within 1 year, or until the salve goes rancid.

B.S. SALVE

There's no bull here! This salve is great for all those bumps and scratches. It is soothing and healing, easing the pain of bumps, bruises, and scratches, breaking down stagnant blood that forms bruises.

2 tablespoons dried plantain leaves

2 tablespoons dried calendula

1½ tablespoons dried lavender flowers

1½ tablespoons dried rose petals

1 tablespoon dried basil

1½ cups olive oil

1½ ounces beeswax

1. Follow the instructions in chapter 3 for making an herb-infused oil and a salve (page 21) using the plantain leaves, calendula, lavender, rose petals, basil, olive oil, and beeswax.

2. Label your salve with the name, ingredient list, and date it was made.

TO USE: Apply liberally as needed to scratches, bumps, and bruises.

VARIATIONS: This can be used as an oil instead of a salve for massaging into bumps and bruises.

STORAGE: Store in a cool, dark location and use within 1 year or until the salve goes rancid.

COUGH CALMER SYRUP

MAKES 3 CUPS

Coughs come in many forms, including a tickling cough; a dry, unproductive cough; and a wet, barking cough. They can also be hot and painful or more on the cold side. This syrup helps clear excess mucus from the lungs, soothing spasmodic coughs for lungs that are full of stuck mucus.

2 tablespoons dried basil

2 tablespoons dried raspberry

2 tablespoons dried peppermint

1 tablespoon dried peach

1 tablespoon dried mullein leaves

½ chopped red onion

1. Follow the instructions in chapter 3 for making a syrup (page 18) using the basil, raspberry, peppermint, peach, mullein, and onion.

2. Label your syrup with the name, ingredient list, and date it was made.

TO USE: Take 1 to 3 teaspoons as needed.

VARIATIONS: If the cough is dry and irritable, swap out the basil for marshmallow root.

STORAGE: Store in the refrigerator and use within 3 months.

CUTS AND SCRAPES DUSTING POWDER

MAKES ABOUT 20 APPLICATIONS

This powder helps clot wounds, keeps germs at bay, helps reduce pain, and helps heal the wound. Because it is a powder, versus a salve or oil, it helps dry out especially weepy wounds.

2 teaspoons powdered echinacea roots

1 teaspoon powdered marshmallow roots

1 teaspoon powdered lavender

1 teaspoon powdered comfrey roots

1 teaspoon powdered calendula

1. In a small bowl, combine the echinacea, marshmallow, lavender, comfrey, and calendula, and stir until well mixed.

2. Pour into a jar with a shaker top (an empty spice jar that's been washed works great), and label with the ingredients and instructions for use.

TO USE: Shake the powder onto a cleaned wound to fill it. If needed, cover with a bandage to hold the powder in place. Apply 2 to 3 times a day or as needed if the wound is weeping.

VARIATIONS: Rose, elderflower, and prunella all make great additions to this wound powder. Use about 1 teaspoon of each and whichever you prefer.

STORAGE: Store in a cool, dry location and use within 1 to 2 years.

ENDURANCE INFUSION

MAKES 8 CUPS

Running a homestead can be an exhausting endeavor. There are always gardens to weed, animals to tend to, and projects to build. This nourishing infusion helps give you the strength and endurance you need to not burn yourself out.

1 cup dried stinging nettles

1 cup dried raspberry leaves

Follow the instructions in chapter 3 for making an infusion (page 17) using the nettles and raspberry leaves.

TO USE: Drink 16 ounces daily.

VARIATIONS: Try adding a pinch of peppermint leaves to sweeten this infusion.

STORAGE: Store in the refrigerator and consume within 4 days.

FENNEL DIGESTIVE PASTILLES

MAKES 10 PASTILLES

These pastilles are great for assisting with the relief of gas, bloating, stomach upsets, and other digestive complaints. Store a small bottle in your purse or bag for on-the-go relief.

1 tablespoon fennel powder, plus more for dusting

2 teaspoons raw honey

1. Put the fennel powder in a small bowl, then drizzle in the honey, stirring to combine as you drizzle. If the mixture forms a stiff paste before you finish, stop drizzling the honey. If it's still sticky and soft, add more powder.

2. Put the additional fennel powder in a separate small bowl.

3. Coat your hands with fennel powder.

4. Pinch off a small piece of the dough, about the size of a pea, and roll it into a ball.

5. Roll the ball in the fennel powder, then store in a glass storage container.

6. Repeat until all the pastilles have been formed.

TO USE: Eat 1 pastille 15 to 20 minutes before a meal for improved digestion. For indigestion, gas, and bloating, take 1 or 2 as needed.

VARIATIONS: You can increase this recipe easily by doubling or tripling the amounts of fennel and honey.

STORAGE: Store in a cool, dry location in an airtight container and use within 2 months.

FIRE CIDER

MAKES 8 CUPS

Fire cider is a traditional recipe made popular by herbalist Rosemary Gladstar. It can be taken daily to keep yourself healthy, or can be taken in larger amounts to help boost your immune system if you feel something coming on. The flavor is sweet and spicy. Use caution when chopping hot peppers, as they can irritate the skin, eyes, and nose. Use gloves or wash your hands thoroughly immediately after chopping.

1 onion

2 to 3 heads garlic

1 (3-inch) piece ginger root

1 (6- to 8-inch) horseradish root

1 or 2 hot peppers such as cayenne or habanero

8 cups apple cider vinegar

2 to 3 cups raw honey

1. Begin by finely chopping up the onion, garlic, ginger root, horseradish root, and hot peppers and placing them in a half-gallon jar.

2. Fill the jar with the vinegar.

3. Cover the jar with a piece of wax paper, then put on the lid.

4. Steep for 4 weeks, shaking daily.

5. After 4 weeks, strain the herbs, reserving the liquid, and compost them.

6. Return the infused vinegar to the jar and add the honey to taste. Some prefer it sweeter, so feel free to adjust the sweetness to your own taste.

TO USE: Take 2 to 3 tablespoons at the first sign of an illness and repeat hourly. As a tonic, take 2 to 3 tablespoons daily. This can also be used as a salad dressing.

VARIATIONS: Add herbs such as elderberries, lemon, rosemary, thyme, sage, lemon balm, turmeric, or nettles to both flavor and increase the medicinal value of fire cider. The additional herbs can be fresh or dried, whatever is available.

STORAGE: Store in a glass jar in a cool, dark location, and your fire cider will last 2 to 3 years.

FLU FIGHTER TEA

MAKES ⅞ CUP LOOSE TEA (14 CUPS BREWED TEA)

When you've got an aching body, wracking headache, fever, chills, and sore throat and just want to sleep but you're too miserable, this tea can help ease the aches and pains and help you sweat out a fever.

¼ cup dried echinacea leaves and flowers

¼ cup dried, crushed rose hips

2 tablespoons dried peppermint

2 tablespoons dried elderflower

1 tablespoon crushed cinnamon stick

1 tablespoon dried yarrow

In a small bowl, combine the echinacea, rose hips, peppermint, elderflower, cinnmaon, and yarrow. Transfer to an airtight container, and label with the ingredients and instructions for use.

TO USE: Steep 1 tablespoon tea blend in 8 ounces of boiling water for 15 to 20 minutes. Drink 1 cup every couple of hours.

VARIATIONS: 2 tablespoons of willow bark can be added to the mix to help with extra aches, but avoid giving it to children under the age of 12.

STORAGE: Store in a cool, dark location and use within 2 years.

HEADACHE HELPER FORMULA

MAKES 2 OUNCES

Headaches are not much fun. They can disrupt the entire day. This blend of herbs helps to soothe a headache fast, letting you get on with your day. Do not give willow internally to children under the age of 18.

1 ounce willow tincture

½ ounce
  peppermint tincture

½ ounce basil tincture

1. Combine the willow tincture, peppermint tinture, and basil tincture in a 1-cup glass measuring cup and mix well.

2. Using a small metal funnel (if you have one), pour the tincture blend into a 2-ounce dropper bottle.

3. Tighten the dropper lid on the bottle, and label with the name of the formula and the dosage information.

TO USE: Add 30 to 60 drops tincture blend to a small glass of water or juice and drink. Repeat every 20 to 30 minutes for up to 2 hours.

VARIATIONS: This blend of herbs can also be combined as a bath tea blend, using 1 cup willow, ½ cup peppermint, and ½ cup basil steeped in ½ gallon of boiling water for 15 to 20 minutes before adding to the bath.

STORAGE: Store the bottle in a cool, dark location.

HIVES HEALER POULTICE

MAKES 1 POULTICE

Hives can be uncomfortable and irritating, especially for children. This poultice helps soothe and reduce hives. Colloidal oatmeal is oatmeal that's been powdered—a blender or coffee grinder make short work of this.

1 tablespoon
colloidal oatmeal

1 tablespoon rhassoul,
bentonite, or French clay

1 teaspoon
powdered chamomile

1 teaspoon
powdered lavender

1 teaspoon powdered rose

1 teaspoon powdered
gotu kola

3 tablespoons
boiling water

1 teaspoon melted
coconut oil

1. In a small bowl, combine the oatmeal, clay, chamomile, lavender, rose, and gotu kola.

2. Stir in the water and coconut oil.

TO USE: Apply the mixture to the hives and let sit until dried. Soak in a warm tub with a muslin bagful of uncooked oatmeal. Soak it in the water, then squeeze the liquid out of the bag onto the hives.

VARIATIONS: If you don't have gotu kola, use 1 teaspoon powdered willow bark.

STORAGE: You can make up a larger batch of this and store it in a glass jar to have on hand. Store in a cool, dark location.

INSECT STING AND BITE RELIEF FORMULA AND COMPRESS

MAKES 4 OUNCES

When stung or bitten by an insect, I like to take a two-pronged approach. I'll apply the remedy directly to the afflicted area and take it internally as well. This allows the herbs to directly soothe the area while also supporting the body to reduce the histamine reaction.

2 ounces peach tincture

1 ounce basil tincture

1 ounce echinacea tincture

1. Combine the peach tincture, basil tincture, and echinacea tincture in a 1-cup glass measuring cup and mix well.

2. Using a small metal funnel (if you have one), pour the tincture blend into a 2-ounce dropper bottle.

3. Tighten the dropper lid on the bottle, and label with the name of the formula and the dosage information.

TO USE: If you have been stung by a bee, be sure to carefully remove the stinger first by using a thin and rigid object such as a fingernail or credit card. Reverse the stinger cut of the skin by pressing at the edge of where the stinger is embedded. That way, when you scrape it out, you are not injecting the venom into your body, which would increase the reaction. Soak a small piece of flannel cloth in the tincture blend and apply it to the wound. Repeat every 20 to 30 minutes or when the cloth feels hot to touch. Internally, add 30 to 60 drops tincture blend to a small glass of water or juice and drink every 20 minutes for 1 to 2 hours, or until the swelling has reduced.

VARIATIONS: In a pinch, a chewed plantain leaf or basil leaf can be applied as a quick spit poultice to the sting or bite.

STORAGE: Store the bottle in a cool, dark location.

ITCHY EYE RELIEF EYE WASH

MAKES 4 CUPS

Allergies, styes, and conjunctivitis can make eyes dry, irritated, and itchy. Use this eye wash formula to help soothe them and encourage healing.

**2 teaspoons
dried elderflower**

**2 teaspoons dried
chamomile**

2 teaspoons dried basil

2 teaspoons dried thyme

In a small bowl, combine the elderflower, chamomile, basil, and thyme. Transfer to an airtight container, and label with the ingredients and directions.

TO USE: Steep 2 teaspoons tea blend in 8 ounces boiling water for 15 to 20 minutes. Add 1 teaspoon of sea salt to the tea as it steeps, stirring to dissolve. Once cooled, strain and pour into an eye cup. Lean forward, placing the eye cup tightly against your eye with your eye open. Sit or stand upright, flip your head back, blink several times, then lean forward again. Rinse the cup with hot, soapy water, then repeat with the other eye, even if it's not affected. Repeat 4 to 5 times daily until the eyes are completely clear of any irritation.

VARIATIONS: Add 2 teaspoons of ground ivy or prunella for extra eye support.

STORAGE: Store the tea blend in a cool, dark location and use within 2 years. The prepared tea can be refrigerated and reheated for use for 3 to 4 days.

LICE LAMBASTER LIQUID

MAKES 4 OUNCES

When lice enter a household, it makes everyone miserable. Applying chemical products can be irritating to the scalp, and they are generally extremely toxic. This oil helps get rid of the lice by suffocating them without the use of harsh chemicals.

1 ounce black walnut-infused oil

1 ounce rosemary-infused oil

1 ounce sage-infused oil

1 ounce fennel-infused oil

1. Combine the black walnut-infused oil, rosemary-infused oil, sage-infused oil, and fennel-infused oil in a glass measuring cup and mix well.

2. Pour into a 4-ounce bottle.

3. Tighten the lid on the bottle and label with the name of the formula and the date made.

TO USE: Apply a liberal amount of oil to the scalp and massage. Cover with a shower cap, and leave on for 30 minutes, then use a lice comb to comb out the scalp. Rinse with warm water followed by shampoo. Repeat as needed.

VARIATIONS: Basil- and peppermint-infused oils can be used in place of the rosemary and sage.

STORAGE: Store in the refrigerator for up to 1 year and discard at the first sign of rancidity.

POISON IVY AND POISON OAK RELIEF

MAKES 4 OUNCES

Nothing is worse than a poison ivy rash when you're out in the hot sun trying to pull weeds. That itch can make you miserable! This spray helps soothe that itch while helping dry out the oils that are under the skin to heal the rash faster. For a quick fix on the itch, run the rash under extremely hot water, as hot as you can stand it (but not hot enough to burn your skin), for about 30 seconds. You'll notice an intense surge of the itch and then it will go away. This is extremely helpful at night for when you're trying to fall asleep. Follow up with a generous dose of this spray.

½ ounce peppermint tincture

½ ounce jewelweed tincture

½ ounce echinacea tincture

½ ounce rosemary-infused vinegar

2 ounces distilled water

1. Combine the peppermint tincture, jewelweed tincture, echinacea tincture, infused vinegar, and water in a 1-cup glass measuring cup and mix well.

2. Pour the tincture into a 4-ounce glass bottle with a spray-top lid.

3. Tighten the lid on the bottle and label with the name of the formula and the usage information.

TO USE: If you've come into contact with poison ivy or poison oak, immediately take a shower and scrub your body with a soapy washcloth vigorously. This helps remove much of the oils and can prevent an outbreak. After drying off, follow up with a good covering of this spray on any exposed areas. If a rash does break out, spray on several times a day to help dry up the rash. If you try the hot-water method to relieve the itch, apply the spray after drying off.

VARIATIONS: If you don't have access to jewelweed, peach leaf tincture can be substituted.

STORAGE: Store the bottle in a cool, dark location.

RINGWORM RELIEF

Black walnut and calendula are top-notch for eliminating ringworm. They work within days of the first application, and this tincture is great to have on hand to reduce the skin fungus.

¾ ounce black walnut hull tincture

¼ ounce calendula tincture

1. Combine the black walnut hull tincture and calendula tincture in a 1-cup glass measuring cup and mix well.

2. Pour the tincture into a 1-ounce glass dropper bottle.

3. Tighten the dropper lid on the bottle, and label with the name of the formula and the dosage information.

TO USE: Apply several drops directly to the ringworm and lightly massage. Repeat 1 to 2 times daily until all trace of the ringworm is gone.

VARIATIONS: If you don't have calendula, you can use straight black walnut. Black walnut leaf can be used if you're worried about staining your skin, but it might take longer to relieve the ringworm. The leaf can also be made as a strong infusion (page 17) and used as a wash on the ringworm in place of tincture. Wash 4 to 6 times daily.

STORAGE: Store the bottle in a cool, dark location.

SINUS SAVER FORMULA

MAKES 4 OUNCES

When you need relief from sinus congestion and pain, this formula can help. The herbs help soothe inflamed membranes, dry up mucus, and reduce infection.

1 ounce echinacea tincture

1 ounce basil tincture

1 ounce peach tincture

½ ounce raspberry tincture

½ ounce dried stinging
  nettles tincture

1. Combine the echinacea tincture, basil tincture, peach tincture, raspberry tincture, and nettles tincture in a 1-cup glass measuring cup and mix well.

2. Pour the tincture into a 4-ounce glass dropper bottle.

3. Tighten the dropper lid on the bottle and label with the name of the formula and the dosage information.

TO USE: Add 30 to 60 drops of the tincture blend to a small glass of water or juice, and drink up to 4 times daily until symptom free for 24 hours.

VARIATIONS: This herb blend can be made into a tea. Combine 1 cup dried echinacea (aerial parts), 1 cup dried basil, 1 cup dried peach leaves, ½ cup dried raspberry leaves, and ½ cup dried stinging nettle leaves. Steep 2 teaspoons tea blend in 8 ounces boiling water for 15 to 20 minutes. Drink in half cups as needed.

STORAGE: Store the bottle in a cool, dark location.

SLEEP TIGHT FORMULA

MAKES 4 OUNCES

Have you ever had a night when you just can't seem to fall asleep? Tossing and turning, lightly drifting off, only to be woken by a noise or twitchy leg? This formula helps turn off chattery thoughts, relax you, and helps you fall asleep. If this is a common occurrence, consider altering your nighttime routine to include a relaxing Epsom salt bath and no electronic devices for at least an hour before bedtime. Regular exercise can also help improve sleep patterns.

1 ounce chamomile tincture

1 ounce lavender tincture

1 ounce rose tincture

1 ounce passionflower tincture

1. Combine the chamomile tincture, lavender tincture, rose tincture, and passionflower tincture in a 1-cup glass measuring cup and mix well.

2. Pour the tincture blend into a 4-ounce glass dropper bottle.

3. Tighten the dropper lid on the bottle and label with the name of the formula and the dosage information.

TO USE: Add 30 to 60 drops tincture blend to a small glass of water or juice and drink before bed, repeating after 20 minutes if needed.

VARIATIONS: If you prefer tea, use this herb blend: Combine 1 cup each of dried chamomile, lavender, rose, and passionflower. Steep 1 tablespoon in 8 ounces boiling water for 15 to 20 minutes. Drink 1 cup as needed.

STORAGE: Store the bottle in a cool, dark location.

SORE THROAT SOOTHER

MAKES 1 CUP LOOSE TEA (24 CUPS BREWED TEA)

Whether it's caused by allergies, a virus, or bacteria, a sore throat is painful. This tea helps reduce inflammation, ease the pain, and heal the throat.

¼ cup dried raspberry leaves

¼ cup dried ginger root pieces

¼ cup dried thyme

2 tablespoons basil

2 tablespoons sage

In a small bowl, combine the raspberry leaves, ginger, thyme, basil, and sage. Transfer to an airtight container, and label with the ingredients and instructions for use.

TO USE: Steep 2 teaspoons of the tea blend in 8 ounces boiling water for 15 to 20 minutes. Add raw honey to sweeten if desired (honey also has healing benefits as long as it is raw). Drink 1 cup as needed.

VARIATIONS: This tea can also be used as a gargle. Simply add 1 teaspoon sea salt to the tea as it steeps, then gargle.

STORAGE: Store in a cool, dark location and use within 2 years.

SPLINTER AND PRICKLE POULTICE

MAKES 1 POULTICE

Splinters, glass slivers, and prickles can become embedded under the skin and hard to remove. This poultice helps draw them to the surface of the skin for easy removal. For deeply embedded splinters, expect to apply this poultice for up to a week to see results.

1 to 2 fresh plantain leaves or 1 teaspoon dried

30 drops peach tincture

1 teaspoon activated charcoal

1. For best results, chew the plantain leaves until they are mashed into a poultice. This provides saliva, which contains healing. If you do not want to chew the poultice, the leaves can be chopped finely and mixed with 1 tablespoon of boiling water, then strained after 15 minutes.

2. In a small bowl, mix the plantain with the tincture and charcoal.

TO USE: Apply directly over the splinter and cover with an adhesive bandage. Repeat every 8 to 12 hours until the splinter has come to the surface and can be removed with tweezers.

VARIATIONS: If peach tincture is not available, substitute with echinacea tincture.

S.o.S. SOAK

MAKES 3 CUPS LOOSE TEA (6 SOAKS)

S.o.S., in this case, stands for "sprains or strains," which can be excruciatingly uncomfortable. This soak helps reduce inflammation and repair damaged tissue while easing pain.

1 cup dried
   raspberry leaves

1 cup dried willow bark

½ cup dried comfrey leaves

½ cup dried lavender

In a small bowl, combine the raspberry leaves, willow, comfrey, and lavender, and mix well. Transfer to an airtight container, and label with the ingredients and instructions for use.

TO USE: While boiling 1 quart of water, put 2 tablespoons of Epsom salt and ½ cup blend into a plastic shoe box or a plastic tub. Add the boiling water to the shoebox and steep until cool enough to put your foot and ankle in the shoe box. Soak for 20 minutes. Repeat the soak 2 to 3 times daily until the sprain or strain is healed.

VARIATIONS: If you are trying to heal a strain or sprain that is not on the ankle, this tea can be used as a compress. Simply soak a piece of flannel or other cloth in the steeped tea and apply it to the sprain for 20 minutes, keeping it warm while it is applied.

STORAGE: Store in a cool, dark location and use within 2 years.

SUNBURN SOOTHER SPRAY

MAKES 4 OUNCES

Prevention is the best medicine, so when you're heading into the sun, be sure to cover up with a thin layer of clothing and a hat! For those times when you forget to do that, this spray helps soothe sunburns, ease the pain from them, and assist in healing the skin. This spray can be used on other burns as well.

½ ounce mullein leaf tincture

½ ounce lavender tincture

½ ounce raspberry leaf-infused vinegar

½ ounce rose petal-infused vinegar

2 ounces distilled water

1. Combine the mullein leaf tincture, lavender tincture, raspberry leaf-infused vinegar, rose petal-infused vinegar, and water in a 1-cup glass measuring cup and mix well.

2. Pour the tincture blend into a 4-ounce glass bottle with a spray-top lid.

3. Tighten the lid on the bottle, and label with the name of the formula and the usage information.

TO USE: Spray on sunburn for relief. Reapply as needed.

VARIATIONS: You may wish to substitute 1 ounce of distilled water with 1 ounce of aloe vera juice.

STORAGE: Store the bottle in a cool, dark location.

TICK AND SPIDER BITE POULTICE

MAKES 1 POULTICE

Tick and spider bites can be scary because of the threat of Lyme disease from ticks and toxic bites from brown recluse spiders. It's always important to have a medical care practitioner check out the bites, but in the meantime, this poultice helps draw the toxins out of your body.

1 to 2 fresh plantain leaves or 1 teaspoon dried

30 drops echinacea tincture

10 drops peach tincture

1 teaspoon activated charcoal

1. For best results, chew the plantain leaves until they are mashed into a poultice. This provides saliva, which contains healing. If you do not want to chew the poultice, the leaves can be chopped finely and mixed with 1 tablespoon of boiling water, then strained after 15 minutes.

2. In a small bowl, mix the plantain with the echinacea tincture, peach tincture, and charcoal.

TO USE: Apply directly over the bite and cover with an adhesive bandage. Repeat every 8 to 12 hours for up to 7 days or until the bite has healed.

VARIATIONS: If you have been bitten by a tick and suspect Lyme disease, adding 30 drops of spilanthes or 10 drops of teasel tincture in a little water or juice, and drinking 3 times daily for a week can help reduce your chances of contracting Lyme disease.

TUMMY TAMER TEA

MAKES 2 CUPS LOOSE TEA (48 CUPS BREWED TEA)

Stomachaches can occur for a variety of reasons. If you've eaten too much or the wrong kind of food and your stomach is protesting, this tea can help reduce digestive pain, relieve gas and bloating, and increase digestive function. It makes a great after-dinner tea.

1 cup dried peppermint

½ cup dried chamomile

¼ cup dried basil

¼ cup fennel seeds

In a small bowl, combine the peppermint, chamomile, basil, and fennel seeds. Transfer to an airtight container, and label with the ingredients and instructions for use.

TO USE: Steep 2 teaspoons of the tea blend in 8 ounces boiling water for 20 to 25 minutes. Drink ½ cup to 1 cup as needed.

VARIATIONS: Don't have any dried basil? You can substitute rosemary or thyme.

STORAGE: Store tea blend in a cool, dark location and use within 2 years.

UTI FORMULA

MAKES 4 OUNCES

This tincture has a strong flavor due to the garlic but is very effective in eliminating urinary tract infections and inflammation. Add it to unsweetened cranberry juice for added benefit, and drink plenty of water to help flush your bladder.

1 ounce echinacea tincture

1 ounce mullein leaf tincture

1 ounce rose petal tincture

½ ounce garlic tincture

½ ounce stinging nettle seed tincture

1. Combine the echinacea tincture, mullein leaf tincture, rose petal tincture, garlic tincture, and stinging nettle seed tincture in a 1-cup glass measuring cup and mix well.

2. Pour the tincture blend into a 4-ounce glass dropper bottle.

3. Tighten the dropper lid on the bottle and label with the name of the formula and the dosage information.

TO USE: Add 30 to 40 drops of the tincture blend to a small glass of water or juice, and drink 4 to 6 times daily. Continue taking for 3 days after all signs of infection are gone.

VARIATIONS: If you don't have garlic tincture, mash 1 garlic clove, and steep it in your tinctures in an airtight jar overnight.

CHAPTER SEVEN

|||||||||||||||||||||||||||||||||||||||||||||||||||||||||||||||||

RECIPES FOR HOUSEKEEPING AND BEAUTY

ALL-PURPOSE KITCHEN AND BATHROOM SURFACE CLEANER

MAKES 16 OUNCES

This cleaner works great for cleaning countertops, refrigerators, and bathroom fixtures. Make up two bottles so you can store one in the kitchen and one in the bathroom.

2 tablespoons dried lavender

2 tablespoons dried rose petals

1 tablespoon dried chamomile

2 cups boiling water

1 teaspoon lavender liquid castile soap

1 teaspoon borax

½ teaspoon washing soda

1. In a 4-cup glass measuring cup or medium glass bowl, steep the lavender, rose petals, and chamomile in the water for 15 to 20 minutes, then strain, reserving the liquid.

2. In a small saucepan, reheat the liquid over medium heat so that it is hot enough to dissolve the washing soda and borax. Stir regularly while heating.

3. Stir in the liquid castile soap, borax, and washing soda.

4. Pour the mixture into a 16-ounce glass bottle with a spray-top lid.

5. Tighten the lid on the bottle and label with the name of the formula and the usage information.

TO USE: Spray on the surface you are cleaning, then wipe off with a sponge or cloth.

VARIATIONS: My favorite castile soap is Dr. Bronner's. If you use this soap, you can choose from a variety of scents, including lavender, rose, and peppermint to add an extra scent to your cleaner.

STORAGE: Store in a cool location.

BASIL AIR-CLEARING HYDROSOL

MAKES 16 OUNCES

Hydrosols are great for spraying in the air, adding flavoring to water, or making a refreshing body or face splash. If you are making this with garden basil, it makes for a delicious spray for food. Spray into the air to "clear the air" and your mind.

4 cups dried basil

4 cups water

Small bag of ice

1. Set up a slow cooker. Place a fire brick in the bottom. Set a small glass bowl in the center, on top of the brick. (A 1-cup glass measuring cup works great for this.)

2. Put the dried basil in the bottom of the slow cooker, being careful not to get it in the glass bowl. The dried basil needs to come to the top of the brick.

3. Pour in enough water to just cover the basil. Set the lid on upside down, with the knob pointing toward the bowl.

4. Set the slow cooker on high. When it heats up, add ice to the top of the lid. This will cool the condensation that will form on the bottom of the lid and help it drip into the bowl. Let it sit for about 5 hours, watching it and checking the water level occasionally. Change the ice when it melts, draining off the water and adding fresh ice. Be careful not to pour any of the melted ice water into the slow cooker.

5. When the water level is nearly at the bottom, it is time to stop. Do not let the water completely leave the bottom of the slow cooker.

CONTINUED ▶

6. Use a hot pad to carefully remove the bowl or glass measuring cup with the hydrosol in it. There will be drops of oil (the essential oil from the basil) floating on top. Pour the contents of the bowl into a bottle and label.

TO USE: Place in a spray bottle to mist the air for cleansing and purifying. Add a tablespoon to a cup of plain water to enhance the flavor.

VARIATIONS: To make a refreshing body splash, mix with equal parts of witch hazel.

STORAGE: Store the hydrosol in the refrigerator to keep it fresh and use within 3 months.

COMFREY FERTILIZER

MAKES 1 TO 2 GALLONS

Comfrey is a versatile plant to have on hand on the homestead. Many animals love to eat it, and besides its healing actions, comfrey is also a great plant fertilizer. Comfrey leaves contain more nitrogen than farmyard manure, and it is high in potassium and phosphorus, too. If you need to heat up your compost quickly, add fresh comfrey leaves to the mix.

Enough fresh comfrey leaves to fill a 5-gallon bucket

1. Fill a 5-gallon bucket with comfrey. Pack the leaves in without crushing them to fill the bucket solidly.

2. Place a brick on top of the leaves to help weigh them down.

3. Seal the bucket closed with a locking lid.

4. Let the bucket sit for 6 weeks in the shade or in full sun. During the summer, the process will complete a bit faster, so check the status after 4 weeks.

5. Strain the leaves and reserve the liquid. Compost the spent comfrey leaves. The liquid is a concentrated form of your fertilizer and it should be dark brown and most likely won't have much of an odor to it.

TO USE: Add 1 part comfrey fertilizer to 10 parts water, then water your plants normally, following their individual recommended fertilizing schedule.

VARIATIONS: If you need a rooting hormone in your fertilizer, add a handful of willow twigs to your bucket, since willow helps plants grow roots.

STORAGE: Store the fertilizer in an old 1-gallon vinegar jug in a cool, dark location.

FURNITURE POLISH

MAKES 8 OUNCES

If you're like me, you have a weakness for beautiful wooden furniture. This natural polish helps keep wooden furniture looking beautiful.

½ cup basil-infused olive oil

¼ cup lemon peel-infused white vinegar

¼ cup lemon juice

1. Combine the oil, vinegar, and lemon juice in a 1-cup glass measuring cup and mix well.

2. Pour the mixture into an 8-ounce glass bottle with a spray-top lid.

3. Tighten the lid on the bottle and label with the name of the formula and the usage information.

TO USE: Spray onto your furniture and wipe off with a soft cloth.

VARIATIONS: If you have dark wood furniture, substitute walnut hull-infused oil for the basil-infused oil.

STORAGE: Store in the refrigerator and use within 6 months.

GLASS CLEANER

MAKES 16 OUNCES

Keep your windows and mirrors sparkling with this natural glass cleaner.

¼ cup basil tincture

¼ cup lavender-infused white vinegar

1 tablespoon arrowroot powder

1½ cups hot water

1. Combine the basil tincture, vinegar, arrowroot, and water in a 4-cup glass measuring cup and mix well.

2. Pour the mixture into a 16-ounce glass bottle with a spray-top lid.

3. Tighten the lid on the bottle and label with the name of the formula and the usage information.

TO USE: Spray onto a glass surface and use a cheesecloth to wipe dry. To reduce streaking, use a sheet of newspaper for a final wipe.

VARIATIONS: Try different tinctures in this recipe, such as rose, peppermint, or sage.

STORAGE: Store in a cool location.

RUG FRESHENER

MAKES 2½ CUPS

This rug freshener helps eliminate odors and also helps keep them free of fleas. Use caution when mixing the diatomaceous earth, and do not breathe it in, since it can be harsh on the lungs.

1 cup borax

1 cup baking soda

½ cup diatomaceous earth

1 teaspoon powdered rosemary

1 teaspoon powdered lavender

1 teaspoon powdered thyme

1. In a medium bowl, combine the borax, baking soda, diatomaceous earth, rosemary, lavender, and thyme, and mix well. (Use caution when mixing diatomaceous earth and do not breathe it in.)

2. Pour into a jar with a shaker top (an empty cheese bottle or a mason jar with holes punched into the lid both work well), and label with the ingredients and instructions for use.

TO USE: Sprinkle the powder heavily over your carpet or rug and let sit for 10 minutes. Vacuum thoroughly.

VARIATIONS: Switch the dried herbs with any herb scents you prefer. This recipe can be made in larger quantities if you have many rugs and carpets to vacuum.

STORAGE: Store in a cool, dry location.

SHOWER MILDEW CLEANER

MAKES 8 OUNCES

I love this cleaner for my shower curtains. I use it daily after my shower to help reduce the buildup of mildew. It works well on shower surrounds and tiles, too.

½ cup white vinegar

2 tablespoons dried rosemary

2 tablespoons dried eucalyptus

½ cup Sal Suds

1. Follow the instructions in chapter 3 for making a vinegar tincture (page 19) using the vinegar, rosemary, and eucalyptus.

2. Strain the herbs from the infused vinegar, add the Sal Suds and mix well.

3. Pour into an 8-ounce glass bottle with a spray-top lid.

4. Tighten the lid on the bottle and label with the name of the formula and the usage information.

TO USE: Shake well and spray onto the shower and curtain surface after showering each day.

VARIATIONS: Lavender, rose petals, sage, and thyme all make great substitutions for the herbs in this recipe.

STORAGE: Store in the bathroom.

STOVETOP CLEANER

MAKES 16 OUNCES

This cleaner is great for removing grease and burnt-on food.

1½ cups water

2 tablespoons dried basil

1 tablespoon dried raspberry leaves

1 tablespoon lemon juice

6 tablespoons liquid dish soap

1. In a small saucepan, bring the water to a boil. Add the basil and raspberry. Turn off the heat and steep for 20 minutes. Strain and return the liquid to the pan. Compost the herbs.

2. Add the lemon juice and dish soap. Mix well.

3. Pour into a 16-ounce glass bottle with a spray-top lid.

4. Tighten the lid on the bottle and label with the name of the formula and the usage information.

TO USE: Shake the bottle before use, then spray onto the stovetop. Let sit for 15 to 20 minutes, then wipe off with a damp cloth.

VARIATIONS: You can vary the herbs you use in this recipe. Other herbs that work really well are lemon balm, sage, thyme, and rosemary.

STORAGE: Store in a cool, dark location.

BODY-MOISTURIZING OIL

MAKES 16 OUNCES

Body oils can be used on the skin after baths and showers, or massaged into the skin before a shower to help lock moisture in.

16 ounces jojoba oil

2 tablespoons dried rose petals

2 tablespoons dried chamomile

2 tablespoons dried lavender

1 tablespoon dried comfrey

1. Follow the instructions in chapter 3 for making an herb-infused oil (page 21) using the jojoba oil, rose petals, chamomile, lavender, and comfrey.

2. Strain the herbs, reserving the liquid. Pour the infused oil into a 16-ounce bottle.

3. Tighten the lid on the bottle and label with the name of the formula and the date made.

TO USE: If applying before a shower, massage into your skin, then continue to massage the oil as you shower. The oil is absorbed by your skin while the excess is washed off, leaving your skin plump and moisturized without feeling overly oily. If applying after a shower, massage a small amount into your skin while still wet and allow your skin to air-dry.

VARIATIONS: If you prefer a less floral scent, substitute the rose, chamomile, and lavender with rosemary, sage, and fennel or go for a more neutral combination of peach, raspberry, and stinging nettles.

STORAGE: Store the bottle in a cool location in your bathroom and use within 6 months.

REFRESHING BODY SPLASH

MAKES 16 OUNCES

Splash this on after a shower for a refreshing, nourishing treatment for your skin.

1 cup boiling water

2 tablespoons dried basil

½ cup peppermint tincture

½ cup aloe vera juice

1. In a small bowl, combine the water and basil and steep for 20 minutes.

2. Strain the basil and return the liquid back to the bowl. Compost the basil.

3. Add the tincture and aloe vera juice. Mix well.

4. Pour into a 16-ounce glass bottle and label with the name of the formula and the date made.

TO USE: Shake the bottle, then pour some into your hand to splash onto your body. Alternately, use a spray bottle to spray it on your body.

VARIATIONS: Substitute thyme, sage, or rosemary for the basil.

STORAGE: Store in the bathroom for quick access or in the refrigerator for a cooler splash.

FLORAL FACIAL TONER

MAKES 12 OUNCES

Toners often have alcohol in them, which can be drying to the face. Without the alcohol, this is a gently balancing toner.

1 cup boiling water

2 tablespoons dried elderflower

¼ cup peach leaves or peach flower-infused vinegar

¼ cup raspberry-infused vinegar

1 teaspoon raw honey

¼ cup aloe vera juice

1. In a small bowl, combine the water and elderflower and steep for 20 minutes.

2. Strain the elderflower, reserving the liquid, and return the liquid to the bowl. Compost the elderflower.

3. Add the peach leaves, raspberry-infused vinegar, honey, and aloe vera juice. Mix well.

4. Pour into a 16-ounce glass bottle and label with the name of the formula and the date made.

TO USE: Apply with a cotton ball to a freshly cleaned face.

VARIATIONS: Use a spray bottle to apply as a cooling facial mist during summertime.

STORAGE: Store in a refrigerator for longer storage or use within 30 days.

HERBAL MOUTHWASH

MAKES 16 OUNCES (ABOUT 122 RINSES)

Mouthwashes can contain a lot of chemicals that aren't needed to help freshen your breath. This mouthwash is simple to make and works great. Once you get the general idea of how to make it, you can experiment with all sorts of flavors.

**2 cups chopped
fresh peppermint**

12 ounces grain alcohol

4 ounces filtered water

1. Follow the instructions in chapter 3 for making an alcohol tincture (page 18) using the peppermint and grain alcohol.

2. Once the tincture is ready, strain the peppermint, reserving the liquid, and pour the tincture into a 16-ounce glass bottle. Compost the peppermint.

3. Tighten the lid on the bottle and label with the name of the remedy and the instructions for use.

TO USE: Put 30 to 60 drops of the tincture into a shot glass, and fill about three-quarters full of water. Swish in the mouth like normal mouthwash.

VARIATIONS: This can also be made with other mints, such as spearmint or chocolate mint. Don't like peppermint? Try using cinnamon sticks, fennel seeds, or anise seeds in place of the peppermint leaves for a more palatable flavor. If you have bleeding gums, add 1 tablespoon of oak bark and 1 tablespoon of echinacea to the jar before adding the mint.

STORAGE: Store the bottle in a cool, dark location.

LUSCIOUS LIP BALM

MAKES 18 TUBES

Lip balm is a must-have on the homestead. This recipe is nourishing to the lips, keeping them soft and chapped free all year round. Buy a container of vitamin E oil gel capsules and prick them with a needle to extract the oil to get the vitamin E needed for the recipe. Stashed in the refrigerator, they will last for several years.

1 tablespoon
dried peppermint

1 tablespoon dried
marshmallow roots

1 tablespoon dried
peach leaves

½ ounce almond oil

½ ounce jojoba oil

1 ounce shea butter

1 ounce beeswax

⅛ teaspoon raw honey

⅛ teaspoon vitamin E oil

1. Follow the instructions in chapter 3 for making an herb-infused oil (page 21) using the peppermint, marshmallow, peach leaves, almond oil, and jojoba oil.

2. In a double boiler, combine the infused oils with the shea butter and beeswax, and heat over high heat until all the solids have melted. Turn off the heat.

3. Add the honey and vitamin E oil. Mix well.

4. Transfer the liquid lip balm to a 1-cup glass measuring cup, from which you can more easily pour the lip balm into the lip balm tubes.

5. Let cool and label.

TO USE: Apply as needed to the lips.

VARIATIONS: Substitute peppermint with other aromatic ingredients, such as lemon balm or coffee beans to change the scent and flavor of the lip balm. If you are suspectable to fever blisters, replace the herbs with lemon balm, prunella, and spilanthes to create a lip balm that helps prevent and heal them.

STORAGE: Store in a cool location.

NATURAL DEODORANT

MAKES 7 OUNCES

If you're concerned about the aluminum in commercial deodorants but find that commercial deodorants without it don't seem to work, try this recipe.

1 tablespoon dried sage

2 teaspoons dried lavender

1 teaspoon dried peppermint

3 tablespoons shea butter

2 tablespoons coconut oil

6 tablespoons arrowroot powder

2 tablespoons bentonite clay

1 tablespoon baking soda

1. Follow the instructions in chapter 3 for making an herb-infused oil (page 21) using the sage, lavender, peppermint, shea butter, and coconut oil.

2. Strain off the herbs and compost them.

3. In a small bowl, combine the arrowroot powder, bentonite clay, and baking soda.

4. Put the infused oil in a mixing bowl, and use an electric mixer or a stand mixer to mix on a low setting.

5. Slowly start adding the powder mixture to the oils, about 2 to 3 tablespoons at a time. Continue mixing until all the powder has been blended in.

6. Using a rubber spatula or a spoon, scrape the deodorant into a wide-mouthed container.

7. Tighten the lid and add a label.

TO USE: Pinch off a pea-sized piece of deodorant and rub it between your thumb and finger to soften it. Spread it directly on your armpit. Repeat for the other side.

VARIATIONS: While the sage is helpful for reducing the sweat and odor, you can also try out other herbs such as rosemary, basil, rose, lemon balm, and fennel. If you find you are sensitive to the addition of baking soda, omit it and add more arrowroot powder to compensate.

STORAGE: Store the container in a cool, dark location.

SAGE-SALT-SODA TOOTH POWDER

MAKES 1 CUP

This natural tooth powder will leave your teeth feeling clean, make your breath fresh, and whiten your teeth.

½ cup fresh sage leaves

¼ cup sea salt

2 tablespoons baking soda

1. Using a mortar and pestle, grind the sage leaves into the sea salt.

2. Spread out the ground salt and sage in a glass baking dish, and put in the oven on the lowest possible setting.

3. Heat for 1 to 2 hours, or until the mixture is hard.

4. Remove from the oven, let cool enough to handle, then spoon back into the mortar and pestle and regrind.

5. Add the baking soda and mix well.

6. Pour into an airtight container and label.

TO USE: Wet your toothbrush, then sprinkle the mixture onto it. Brush your teeth as normal, then follow up with Herbal Mouthwash (page 134).

VARIATIONS: You can add 2 tablespoons cinnamon powder after baking or 2 tablespoons of fennel seeds in step 4 to sweeten the flavor a bit.

STORAGE: Store the container in a dry, dark location.

CHAPTER EIGHT

RECIPES FOR PETS AND LIVESTOCK

The following are a few of my tried-and-true recipes for the animals on the homestead. I am only including animals that I've personally raised and used herbs on.

Dosing animals is similar to humans: The dose is dependent on their body weight. Unless noted in the individual recipes, the following are general rules for dosing:

TINCTURES:

3 TO 7 POUNDS: 4 drops

8 TO 15 POUNDS: 5 to 8 drops

16 TO 35 POUNDS: 10 to 12 drops

36 TO 85 POUNDS: 15 to 18 drops

86 TO 150 POUNDS: 20 to 25 drops

150+ POUNDS: 30 to 45 drops

POWDERED HERBS:

LESS THAN 3 POUNDS: ¼ teaspoon

3 TO 7 POUNDS: ½ teaspoon

8 TO 15 POUNDS: ¾ teaspoon

16 TO 35 POUNDS: 1 to 2 teaspoons

36 TO 85 POUNDS: 2 to 3 teaspoons

86 TO 150 POUNDS: 1 to 2 tablespoons

150+ POUNDS: 3 to 4 tablespoons

IMMUNE-BUILDING TONIC

MAKES 8 OUNCES

Access to fresh water, a variety of vegetation (or proper kibble for dogs and cats), a clean area for bedding down at night, and plenty of outdoor space to move around during the day are essential cornerstones for creating a healthy environment for your livestock and to ensure a strong immune system. Sometimes though, they may need some extra help. This formula helps build their immune strength.

5 pokeberries

2 ounces elderberry tincture

2 ounces echinacea tincture

1 ounce garlic tincture

1 ounce raspberry leaf tincture

1. Mash the pokeberries in a 1-cup glass measuring cup, then add the elderberry tincture, echinacea tincture, garlic tincture, raspberry leaf tincture, and mix well.

2. Strain the seeds, reserving the liquid, and pour the tinctures into an 8-ounce glass dropper bottle. Compost the seeds and plant material left in the strainer.

3. Tighten the dropper lid on the bottle and label with the name of the formula and dosage information.

TO USE: Add 1 tablespoon of tincture to your animals' water bowl twice daily for larger animals, such as goats or sheep, or 1 to 2 teaspoons for smaller animals, such as fowl and rabbits. You can add it to a bottle if you are bottle-feeding.

STORAGE: Store the bottle in a cool, dark location.

FLIES-B-GONE SPRAY

MAKES 16 OUNCES

During the summer, flies can be especially annoying for animals that are outside grazing. Use this spray daily to help deter pesky flies and often painful bites. *Do not spray in animals' eyes. For external use only.*

2 ounces elder
  leaf tincture

2 ounces basil tincture

1½ ounces peppermint
  tincture

1½ ounces catnip tincture

1 ounce lemon balm
  tincture

8 ounces distilled water

1. Combine the elder leaf tincture, basil tincture, peppermint tincture, catnip tincture, and lemon balm tincture in a 1-cup glass measuring cup and mix well.

2. Pour the tinctures into a 16-ounce glass spray bottle.

3. Add the distilled water to fill the bottle.

4. Tighten the spray lid on the bottle and label with the name of the formula and instructions for use.

TO USE: Shake well, then spray over the length of your animal's body, avoiding their eyes. To protect their eye area, spray some of the formula onto a cloth and wipe around their eyes.

STORAGE: Store bottle in a cool location.

WHAT-A-PAIN (RELIEVER)

MAKES 4 OUNCES

This formula can be used on humans, but it is formulated for animals. This combination of herbs creates a multidimensional formula that not only helps ease pain but also supports the nervous system to help your animals deal with the stress of pain and injury. Valerian, wild lettuce, California poppy, Saint John's wort, and willow all relieve pain; goldenrod, Saint John's wort, licorice, and willow reduce inflammation. California poppy, valerian, and wild lettuce are sedating, while California poppy, licorice, Saint John's wort, and valerian ease anxiety and calm the nerves. Valerian, goldenrod, California poppy, and licorice ease muscle spasms. Additionally, licorice adds a sweetness to the formula.

1 ounce valerian tincture

1 ounce willow tincture

1 ounce Saint John's wort tincture

¼ ounce California poppy tincture

¼ ounce wild lettuce tincture

¼ ounce goldenrod tincture

¼ ounce licorice root tincture

1. Combine the valerian tincture, willow tincture, Saint John's wort tincture, poppy tincture, lettuce tincture, goldenrod tincture, and licorice tincture in a 1-cup glass measuring cup and mix well.

2. Pour the tinctures into a 4-ounce glass dropper bottle.

3. Tighten the dropper lid on the bottle, and label with the name of the formula and dosage information.

TO USE: Add the tincture blend to your animal's water bowl or bottle (if bottle-feeding), adding only enough water so that you can refill 2 to 3 times in the day with a new dose of the formula. See the chart at the beginning of this chapter for the amount to add according to the size of your animal. In an acute situation, the tincture can be given every 30 to 60 minutes. If they are eating, add the dose to a piece of bread for quicker dosing. If they are not eating, add the tincture to enough water to fill a syringe to drench your animal (be sure to remove the needle before drenching).

STORAGE: Store the dropper bottle in a dark cabinet away from heat.

WORM FORMULA

MAKES 4 CUPS

This formula is extremely strong and should only be given when your animals have worms or every 8 weeks to prevent a recurrence of a parasite infection. Once they are clear of worms, switch to the Worm Between—Maintenance (page 145). The combination of the two wormers must be used year-round for it to be effective. If, for whatever reason, you cannot keep up with the schedule, do not rely on the two formulas to keep your animals worm free. This wormer works by expelling worms from the digestive tract and works on any worms that are found there.

1 cup powdered black walnut hull

1 cup powdered wormwood

½ cup powdered garlic

½ cup powdered fennel

¼ cup powdered cloves

¼ cup powdered tobacco (homegrown is best)

¼ cup powdered stinging nettles

¼ cup powdered tansy

1. In a medium bowl, combine the powdered black walnut hull, wormwood, garlic, fennel, cloves, tobacco, nettles, and tansy, and stir until well mixed.

2. Pour the mixture into a quart jar and label with the ingredients and instructions.

TO USE: Give 1 dose daily for 3 days. Repeat every 8 weeks. For easier dosing, mix with molasses for ruminants, peanut butter for dogs, tuna for cats, or cooked oats for rabbits and fowl. See the chart at the beginning of this chapter for the amount to add according to the size of your animal.

STORAGE: Store the jar in a cool, dry location.

WORM BETWEEN—MAINTENANCE

MAKES 7 CUPS

The Worm Between—Maintenance is given when the Worm Formula (page 144) is not being given. The combination of the two wormers must be used year-round for it to be effective. If, for whatever reason, you cannot keep up with the schedule, do not rely on the two formulas to keep your animals worm free. This maintenance formula works to continue keeping the digestive tract inhospitable for parasites.

1 cup powdered black walnut hull

1 cup powdered garlic

1 cup powdered peach leaves

1 cup powdered pumpkin seeds

1 cup powdered stinging nettles

¾ cup powdered fennel

¾ cup powdered mugwort

½ cup powdered thyme

1. In a medium bowl, combine the powdered black walnut hull, garlic, peach leaves, pumpkin seeds, nettles, fennel, mugwort, and thyme, and stir until well mixed.

2. Pour the mixture into a half-gallon jar and label with the ingredients and instructions.

TO USE: Give 1 dose once a week for 7 weeks. On week 8, switch to Worm Formula. For easier dosing, mix with molasses for ruminants, peanut butter for dogs, tuna for cats, or cooked oats for rabbits and fowl. See the chart at the beginning of this chapter for the amount to add according to the size of your animal.

STORAGE: Store the jar in a cool, dry location.

WOUND POWDER

MAKES ½ CUP

Wound powders are an easy way to help dry up weepy wounds that don't like to heal. Because this is a powder instead of a salve, it sticks better to the wound, making it ideal for those spots that are impossible to bandage. Because this powder is all natural, if your animal licks it off, there is no harm done, as it's safe for consumption.

1 tablespoon powdered echinacea

1 tablespoon powdered chamomile

1 tablespoon powdered rose petals

1 tablespoon powdered lavender

1 tablespoon powdered marshmallow roots

1 tablespoon powdered black walnut leaves

1 tablespoon powdered comfrey leaves

1 tablespoon powdered willow bark

1. In a small bowl, combine the powdered echinacea, chamomile, rose petals, lavender, marshmallow roots, walnut leaves, comfrey leaves, and willow bark, and stir until well mixed.

2. Pour into a jar with a shaker top (an empty cheese bottle or a mason jar with holes punched into the lid both work well) and label with the ingredients and instructions for use.

TO USE: Clean the wound and remove any excess debris. Sprinkle a thick layer of the powder into the wound, gently patting it into place. Repeat 2 to 3 times daily or when wound begins to weep again.

STORAGE: Store the powder container in a cool location.

BEE BALM MITE RELIEF

MAKES 5 CUPS

Varroa mites are one of honeybees' worst enemies and they can quickly destroy a hive. This powder works in two ways. First, the garlic helps stun and repel the varroa mites. Second, the powdered sugar adheres to the backs of the bees, encouraging them to groom themselves and each other, knocking the mites off.

1 pound powdered sugar

1 cup powdered garlic

1. In a medium bowl, combine the sugar and garlic, and stir until well mixed.

2. Pour into a jar and label with the remedy name, ingredients, and instructions for use.

TO USE: Once you have opened your hive, pour the mixture into a flour sifter. Pull the frames out one by one, and shake-sprinkle the mite relief thoroughly on both sides, covering the bees. Repeat until all the frames have been powdered. This should be done once every season (spring, summer, and fall) and repeated once more in the fall since the mites are typically worse at that time of year.

STORAGE: Store the jar in the refrigerator or freezer.

NATURAL SMOKER BLEND

MAKES ENOUGH FOR 1 SMOKE

We were taught this recipe by a local beekeeper who mentored us when we first started raising bees. It makes a great smoke blend that keeps bees calm when it's time to work the hive. The beekeeper also felt that it helped keep the varroa mite population in check.

Handful dry pine needles

Handful sumac berries

1 small plug of twist tobacco, or other natural or additive-free tobacco

3 or 4 pine cones

TO USE: Light the pine needles and, once they are burning, push them into the smoker. Add a thick layer of sumac, the plug of tobacco, a broken-up pine cone, then add more pine needles. Continue packing in layers of pine needles, sumac, and pine cones until the smoker is full.

MITE MANAGER POWDER

MAKES A 1-MONTH SUPPLY

Mites seem to be the most bothersome ailment for fowl, at least in my experience. Our turkeys never seemed bothered by them, but the chickens sometimes were. Chickens often take matters into their own wings by having regular dust baths. You can help them along by sprinkling this powder in their coop to help reduce mites that come into the coop with them. Use caution when mixing the diatomaceous earth, and do not breathe it in since it can be harsh on the lungs.

1 pound
  diatomaceous earth

2 cups powdered
  basil leaves

1 cup powdered garlic

1 cup powdered
  peppermint leaves

1. Combine the diatomaceous earth, basil, garlic, and peppermint, and stir until well mixed. (Use caution when mixing diatomaceous earth and do not breathe it in.)

2. Pour the mixture into a gallon bucket that has a sealable lid and label with the ingredients and instructions.

TO USE: Use a scoop or clean, empty food can to sprinkle the mixture over your chicken coop floor. If they have a favorite dusting spot outdoors, add a bit of the mixture to that area as well. Repeat twice weekly until mites are gone, then reduce to once weekly.

VARIATIONS: Other aromatic herbs such as sage, lavender, rosemary, thyme, tansy, bergamot, and catnip can be used in place of any of these herbs.

STORAGE: Store in a cool location.

SCALY LEG MITE CONTROL

MAKES 4 OUNCES (EACH PART)

Scaly leg mites attach to the feet of fowl, making them look deformed and lumpy and your fowl unable to walk. Start this regimen for your affected fowl the moment you notice it happening for a speedy recovery.

FOR SOLUTION 1

1 ounce garlic-infused vinegar

1 ounce thyme-infused vinegar

1 ounce rosemary-infused vinegar

1 ounce black walnut hull-infused vinegar

FOR SOLUTION 2

1 ounce garlic-infused olive oil

1 ounce thyme-infused olive oil

1 ounce rosemary-infused olive oil

1 ounce black walnut hull-infused olive oil

TO MAKE SOLUTION 1

1. Combine all the vinegars in a 1-cup glass measuring cup and mix well.

2. Pour into a 4-ounce bottle and label with the remedy name and directions.

TO MAKE SOLUTION 2

3. Combine all the oils in a 1-cup glass measuring cup and mix well.

4. Pour into a 4-ounce bottle and label with the remedy name and directions.

TO USE: Fill a gallon bucket or other similarly sized container one-third full of warm water. Add 1 teaspoon natural dish soap and 2 ounces of solution 1. Stir together to combine. One by one, dip your chickens' feet into the solution, holding them there briefly, then use a soft cloth to gently wipe their legs and feet dry, being careful not to harm their scales. Next, soak a clean, old cloth with the oil and gently rub it down the length of their legs and over their feet, making sure the oil thoroughly covers the affected spots.

VARIATIONS: This oil can also be made into a salve following the instructions in chapter 3 (page 21) for easier application.

STORAGE: Store the bottles in a cool location and use within 1 year.

DRY SKIN OIL

MAKES 16 OUNCES (SERVES 32)

Late winter is a time of lots of scratching due to dry skin. The addition of this oil to your dog's food can help relieve the itching.

8 ounces marshmallow root-infused olive oil

4 ounces rose hip-infused olive oil

4 ounces stinging nettle-leaf-infused olive oil

1. In a large glass bowl, combine the marshmallow root–infused oil, rose hip–infused oil, and stinging nettle–infused oil, and mix well.

2. Pour into a 16-ounce bottle.

3. Tighten the lid on the bottle and label with the name of the formula and the date made.

TO USE: Twice daily, add 1 tablespoon of the oil to your dog's food and mix well. For dogs less than 30 pounds, decrease to 1½ teaspoons and for dogs more than 100 pounds, increase to 2 tablespoons.

VARIATIONS: If your dog isn't enthused about the olive oil on their food, try infusing with bacon grease, lard, or tallow instead of olive oil.

STORAGE: Store the bottle in the refrigerator and use within 6 months.

FLEA-FIGHTER FORMULA

MAKES 4 OUNCES

Fleas can make a pet miserable, and once one pet gets fleas, typically all the rest do, too. This formula is added to your pet's daily food, helping change the taste of their blood, making them undesirable to fleas.

1 ounce garlic tincture

½ ounce fennel tincture

½ ounce goldenrod tincture

½ ounce stinging nettles tincture

½ ounce yellow dock tincture

¼ ounce mugwort tincture

¼ ounce peach leaf tincture

¼ ounce neem tincture

¼ ounce rue tincture

1. Combine the garlic tincture, fennel tincture, goldenrod tincture, stinging nettles tincture, yellow dock tincture, mugwort tincture, peach tincture, neem tincture, and rue tincture in a 1-cup glass measuring cup and mix well.

2. Pour the tinctures into a 4-ounce glass dropper bottle.

3. Tighten the dropper lid on the bottle and label with the name of the formula and dosage information.

TO USE: Follow the dosing chart at the beginning of this chapter to determine the dosage for your pet. Start with half of the dose, adding the formula to each pet's food twice daily. After 1 week, increase to the full dose twice daily.

STORAGE: Store the bottle in a cool, dark location.

FLEA-FIGHTER POWDER

MAKES 2 CUPS

Part of the flea battle is eliminating the fleas from your house as well. Use this powder to sprinkle on their bedding, carpets, and wood floors. Use caution when mixing the diatomaceous earth, and do not breathe it in as it can be harsh on the lungs.

1 cup diatomaceous earth

¼ cup
  powdered peppermint

¼ cup powdered lavender

¼ cup powdered basil

¼ cup powdered tansy

1. In a small bowl, combine the diatomaceous earth, peppermint, lavender, basil, and tansy, and stir until well mixed. (Use caution when mixing diatomaceous earth and do not breathe it in.)

2. Pour into a jar with a shaker top (an empty cheese bottle or a mason jar with holes punched into the lid both work well), and label with the ingredients and instructions for use.

TO USE: Sprinkle the powder onto the bedding, carpet, and rugs. Use a broom to help brush into the textiles. Vacuum off after 30 minutes. Sprinkle over wood floors and brush into the cracks, vacuuming out after 30 minutes. Use to dust your pet, being careful not to let them breathe in the mixture and do not sprinkle it near their eyes.

VARIATIONS: If you don't have access to tansy, you can use powdered garlic.

STORAGE: Store in a cool location.

GOAT BLOAT DRENCH

MAKES 1 DRENCH

Goats and sheep have very sensitive digestive systems that are triggered by a variety of factors, including being moved to a new location, having too much grain in their diets, and even eating too many fresh, leafy grains. I like to keep a dish of baking soda available to them to freely eat from, and I find they know when they need a bit to help combat digestive gas from building. In times when that doesn't work out, this drench helps relieve the excess bloating, known as frothy bloat. The addition of soapwort- or soap nut-infused oil enlarges smaller gas bubbles to help the goat burp the gas out.

3 ounces fennel seed-infused olive oil

2 ounces peppermint-infused olive oil

2 ounces chamomile-infused olive oil

1 ounce soapwort- or soap nut-infused olive oil

1. In a small glass bowl, combine the fennel seed-infused oil, peppermint-infused oil, chamomile-infused oil, and soapwort-infused oil, and mix well.

2. Pour into an 8-ounce bottle.

3. Tighten the lid on the bottle and label with the name of the formula and the date made.

TO USE: Depending on your sheep's or goat's weight, drench with 3½ to 6½ ounces (100 to 200 mL) of the mixture. Smaller pygmy goats will need only 3½ ounces (100 mL), whereas larger goats such as angoras and alpines will need 6½ ounces (200 mL). Once you have drenched your animal, walk the animal around, going up slopes if possible, to help encourage the expulsion of gas. If your animal is lying down, rolling the animal a few times and massaging the rumen can help break up the bubbles.

VARIATIONS: If you don't have access to soapwort or soap nuts, substitute 1 ounce of natural dish soap.

STORAGE: Make this ahead of time and store in the refrigerator so you have it on hand. It will store for about 1 year in the refrigerator.

MILK MAKER MASTITIS RELIEF

MAKES 2 OUNCES

Some goats can be prone to mastitis because they produce more milk than their babies can consume. Even when they are being milked regularly, sometimes they become engorged and get mastitis. This formula helps quickly relieve the mastitis.

1 ounce garlic tincture

¾ ounce echinacea tincture

¼ ounce poke root tincture

1. Combine the garlic tincture, echinacea tincture, and poke root tincture in a 1-cup glass measuring cup and mix well.

2. Pour the tincture into a 2-ounce glass dropper bottle.

3. Tighten the dropper lid on the bottle and label with the name of the formula and the dosage information.

TO USE: Add 30 drops tincture to your doe's grain ration twice daily when you are milking her. If mastitis is severe, increase dose to 4 times daily and give the remaining 2 doses in a small handful of grain.

VARIATIONS: If your goat refuses to eat the grain with this formula on it, you can add it to a bit of water and use a drencher to squirt it into her mouth.

STORAGE: Store the bottle in a cool location.

RESOURCES

||||||||||||||||||||||||||||||||||||||||||||||||||||||||||||||||||||||||||||||||||||||||||||||||||||||

MY FAVORITE ONLINE RESOURCES FOR DRIED HERBS AND TINCTURES

MOUNTAIN ROSE HERBS (mountainroseherbs.com)

Mountain Rose Herbs offers a variety of products for herbal medicine-making needs: high-quality herbs, oils and butters, containers, seeds, and even tinctures and infused oils.

PACIFIC BOTANICALS (PacificBotanicals.com)

Another great source for high-quality herbs.

HERBALIST & ALCHEMIST (Herbalist-Alchemist.com)

Ready-made tinctures for adults and children. If I'm unable to make a tincture myself, this is my number one resource to purchase from.

HERB PHARM (Herb-Pharm.com)

High-quality liquid herbal products for the whole family. This is another source I purchase from if I cannot make the tinctures myself.

MY FAVORITE ONLINE RESOURCES FOR HERB PLANTS AND SEEDS

COMPANION PLANTS (CompanionPlants.com)

If you want to grow plants, this is a great place to find bare root plants.

STRICTLY MEDICINAL SEEDS (StrictlyMedicinalSeeds.com)

Richo Cech and his wife specialize in medicinal herb seeds and plants with a huge selection to choose from.

THYME GARDEN HERB CO. (ThymeGarden.com)

Another great source for seeds and some plants as well.

BOOKS AND MAGAZINES FOR HOLISTIC ANIMAL CARE

The Complete Herbal Handbook for the Dog and Cat and *The Complete Herbal Handbook for Farm and Stable* by Juliette de Baïracli Levy

Holistic Goat Care: A Comprehensive Guide to Raising Healthy Animals, Preventing Common Ailments, and Troubleshooting Problems by Gianaclis Caldwell

The Homesteader's Natural Chicken Keeping Handbook: Raising a Healthy Flock from Start to Finish by Amy K. Fewell

WEBSITES

AMERICAN HERBALISTS GUILD (AmericanHerbalistsGuild.com)

A great educational resource for new and experienced herbalists. You can find a registered herbalist in your area if you'd like to work with a qualified herbalist, herb schools around the country if you are interested in getting a more formal education, and lots of learning resources on the website.

AMERICAN BOTANICAL COUNCIL (ABC.HerbalGram.org)

A great resource for learning what's going on in the world of herbal medicine.

HERBAL ROOTS ZINE (HerbalRootszine.com)

This is my herbal PDF publication started in 2009, featuring more than 130 different issues, each focusing on one herb. Each issue is packed with activities to make learning about herbs fun. I also offer online courses for kids and their parents on my website.

SUSTAINABLE HERBS PROGRAM (SustainableHerbsProject.com)

Learn more about the sustainable growth and supply of medicinal herbs in the commercial market.

UNITED PLANT SAVERS (UnitedPlantSavers.org)

Committed to saving our native endangered herbs, this is a great organization that teaches what you can do to help save our fragile plants.

REFERENCE

Griggs, Barbara. *Green Pharmacy: The History and Evolution of Western Herbal Medicine*. Rochester, VT: Healing Arts Press, 1997.

INDEX

||||||||||||||||||||||||||||||||

AILMENT INDEX

Coughs, hacking
  Cough Calmer Syrup
    recipe, 97
  Mullein leaf, 44–45
Coughs, wet and spasmodic
  Cough Calmer Syrup
    recipe, 97
  Thyme, 60–61
Cramps, menstrual
  Barn Cat Balm recipe, 95
  Chamomile, 28–29
  Fennel, 36–37
  Raspberry, 52–53
Cuts, scratches, scrapes
  B.S. Salve recipe, 96
  Cuts and Scrapes Dusting
    Powder recipe, 98
  Comfrey, 30–31
  Elderflower, 34–35
  Marshmallow, 42–43

D

Dairy intolerance
  Basil, 24–25
Delayed menses
  Basil, 24–25
  Sage, 56–57
Dementia, reduces agitation in
  Lavender, 40–41
Diabetes
  Elderflower, 34–35
  Garlic, 38–39
Diarrhea
  Black walnut, 26–27
  Peach, 48–49
  Raspberry, 52–53
  Rose, 54–55
Digestion, increases
  Lavender, 40–41
  Peach Shrub recipe, 79
  Peppermint, 50–51
  Rose, 54–55
  Sage, 56–57

Sage Blossom Vinegar
  recipe, 84–85
Sauerkraut recipe, 86–87
Tummy Tamer Tea
  recipe, 117
Digestive issues
  Basil, 24–25
  Chamomile, 28–29
  Comfrey, 30–31
  Fennel, 36–37
  Fennel Digestive Pastilles
    recipe, 100
  Marshmallow, 42–43
  Peppermint, 50–51
  Tummy Tamer Tea
    recipe, 117
Diverticulosis
  Peppermint, 50–51
Dry, itchy skin
  Comfrey, 30–31

E

Ear infections
  Garlic, 38–39
  Mullein flower, 44–45
Earaches
  Garlic, 38–39
  Mullein flower, 44–45
Earwax, buildup
  Mullein flower, 44–45
Eczema
  Chamomile, 28–29
Electric shock
  Black walnut, 26–27
Emphysema
  Fennel, 36–37
Estrogen production, increases
  Sage, 56–57
Eyes, cataracts
  Fennel, 36–37
Eyes, inflamed
  Fennel, 36–37
  Itchy Eye Relief Eye Wash
    recipe, 106

Eyes, irritated
  Chamomile, 28–29
  Fennel, 36–37
  Itchy Eye Relief Eye Wash
    recipe, 106
  Marshmallow, 42–43
  Rose, 54–55
Eyes, itchy
  Allergy Relief Tea
    recipe, 94
  Chamomile, 28–29
  Itchy Eye Relief Eye Wash
    recipe, 106
  Marshmallow, 42–43
Eyes, sore
  Itchy Eye Relief Eye Wash
    recipe, 106
  Rose, 54–55
Exhaustion
  Endurance Infusion
    recipe, 99

F

Face, oily
  Elderflower, 34–35
False labor pains
  Chamomile, 28–29
Fatigue
  Endurance Infusion
    recipe, 99
Fertility, increase in men
  Raspberry, 52–53
Fever blisters
  Elderberry, 34–35
  Marshmallow, 42–43
Fevers
  Basil, 24–25
  Chamomile, 28–29
  Echinacea, 32–33
  Elderflower, 34–35
  Flu Fighter Tea
    recipe, 102
  Garlic, 38–39

Pertussis
  Garlic, 38–39
  Marshmallow, 42–43
  Peach, 48–49
Pharyngitis
  Sage, 56–57
Phlegm, excess in lungs
  Basil, 24–25
  Elderberry, 34–35
  Mullein leaf, 44–45
  Onion, 46–47
Phlegm, thin out
  Garlic, 38–39
  Mullein leaf, 44–45
  Onion, 46–47
Pneumonia
  Garlic, 38–39
  Mullein leaf, 44–45
  Thyme, 60–61
Poison Ivy/Oak
  Poison Ivy/Oak Relief
    recipe, 108
Poisoning, heavy metal
  Garlic, 38–39
Prostate issues
  Stinging nettles
    root, 58–59
Prostate toning
  Raspberry, 52–53
Psoriasis
  Chamomile, 28–29
  Marshmallow, 42–43

R
Radiation burns
  Chamomile, 28–29
Repellent, mice, rats, voles,
    spiders
  Peppermint, 50–51
Respiratory ailments,
    moist
  Raspberry, 52–53

Respiratory ailments,
    hot and dry
  Marshmallow, 42–43
Rheumatism
  Elderflower, 34–35
  Peppermint, 50–51
  Willow, 62–63
Ringworm
  Black walnut, 26–27
  Garlic, 38–39
  Ringworm Relief
    recipe, 109

S
Saliva, reduces
  Sage, 56–57
Septic infections
  Echinacea, 32–33
Septicemia
  Echinacea, 32–33
Scar tissue
  Comfrey root, 30–31
Scarring, reduction
  Comfrey, 30–31
  Raspberry, 52–53
Sciatica
  Chamomile, 28–29
Scratches
  B.S. Salve recipe, 96
Seasonal affective disorder
  Basil, 24–25
Shingles
  Black walnut, 26–27
Shortness of breath
  Fennel, 36–37
Sinus infection
  Echinacea, 32–33
  Sinus Saver Formula
    recipe, 110
Skin, dry and itchy
  Basil-Infused Oil
    recipe, 66
  Comfrey, 30–31

Dry Skin Oil recipe, 151
  Poison Ivy/Oak Relief
    recipe, 108
Skin, inflammation
  Chamomile, 28–29
Skin, irritations
  Chamomile, 28–29
Sleep, encourages deep
  Chamomile, 28–29
  Sleep Tight Formula
    recipe, 111
Slipped discs
  Mullein root, 44–45
Snake bites
  Echinacea, 32–33
Sneezing, due to allergies
  Allergy Relief Tea
    recipe, 94
Sore throat
  Allergy Relief Tea
    recipe, 94
  Chai Honey recipe, 68
  Echinacea, 32–33
  Elderberry, 34–35
  Flu Fighter Tea
    recipe, 102
  Marshmallow, 42–43
  Raspberry, 52–53
  Rose, 54–55
  Sage, 56–57
  Sage Blossom Vinegar
    recipe, 84–85
  Sore Throat Soother
    recipe, 112
  Thyme, 60–61
Sores
  Onion, 46–47
  Rose, 54–55
Sores, mouth
  Rose, 54–55
  Sage, 56–57
Spasms, bladder
  Marshmallow, 42–43

ACKNOWLEDGMENTS

||||||||||||||||||||||||||||||||||||||||||||||||||||||||||||||||||||||||||||||||||||||||||||||||||||||||||||||||||||||||||||||||||||||||||||||||||||

There are so many wonderful people to acknowledge and thank who have helped me on my homestead and herbal journey.

My first teachers about homesteading and self-sufficiency: my mom and dad. I'll never forget the canning sprees, butchering days, or apple harvests.

My grandmother, Avis Hazel Russell, who also taught me many lessons in self-sufficiency, sewing, and life in general.

My partner, Greg, who agreed to move to this small patch of land and try our hand at homesteading. It's been a wild fifteen years on the homestead!

My partner in homesteading shenanigans, Rebekah Dawn. Plant swapping, goat sharing, hula hooping, and work exchanging have kept us both sane over the years.

All the WWOOFers who came and helped us over the years, but especially Colleen Jordan, for her tireless efforts and hours upon hours of hard work.

A huge thanks to Merryl Winstein of Alpine Dairy and Tori Tilton of Share the Soap for all their help with all the aspects of rearing goats, from breeding to worming, and making cheese and soap.

ABOUT THE AUTHOR

KRISTINE BROWN, RH (AHG), is a practicing traditional community herbalist and mother of four children and two stepchildren, two of whom she homeschooled for eleven years. She studied with Rosemary Gladstar of Sage Mountain and has spent countless hours of independent research and study with herbalists such as Jim McDonald, Leslie Alexander, Leslie Williams, Isla Burgess, Gail Faith Edwards, and Kat Maier. She has taught classes locally since 2004, presented at herbal conferences around the country, and coordinated numerous herbal kids' camps both locally and nationally. She also assists Leslie Alexander, Ph.D., RH (AHG), with the American Herbalist Guild Symposium's Herbal Activity Hub. Kristine is vice president of her local AHG chapter and is very active in her local herbal community. She is the writer and illustrator of the online children's publication *Herbal Roots zine,* which has been published since 2009. Teaching others about herbs and sharing her knowledge with children—our future—is her passion. Kristine lives on a homestead with her partner, their two youngest children, cats, dogs, chickens, goats, and bearded dragon.

www.ingramcontent.com/pod-product-compliance
Lightning Source LLC
Chambersburg PA
CBHW060859090426
42737CB00024B/3493

* 9 7 8 1 6 4 7 3 9 3 7 2 4 *